LECTURES IN ECONOMICS

Marxian Economic Theory

Meghnad Desai

London School of Economics and Political Science

GRAY-MILLS PUBLISHING LTD.
10 Juer Street
London S.W. 11

Printed in Great Britain by
Lowe & Brydone (Printers) Ltd, Haverhill, Suffolk

CONTENTS

Preface

List of algebraic symbols

Chapter

For the last few years, Professor Peter Wiles and I have been jointly giving a course on Marxian Economics. Whereas he deals with the young Marx and the analysis of full communism, I concentrate on Marx's critique of capitalism. This book is an extended and revised version of my contribution to that course.

Many students have advanced my understanding of Marx and taught me to rethink old ideas. I am grateful to E. Akat, Dada Yaffe, Stephen Lord, Peter Nore and Nat Levy among others. Mark Blaug and Gail Wilson read the earlier versions and improved it in several ways. I am also grateful to Geraldine Preece, Carol Martin and Anne de Sayrah for typing the earlier versions.

Meghnad Desai

London School of Economics, 1973

THE THREE CIRCUITS OF CAPITAL

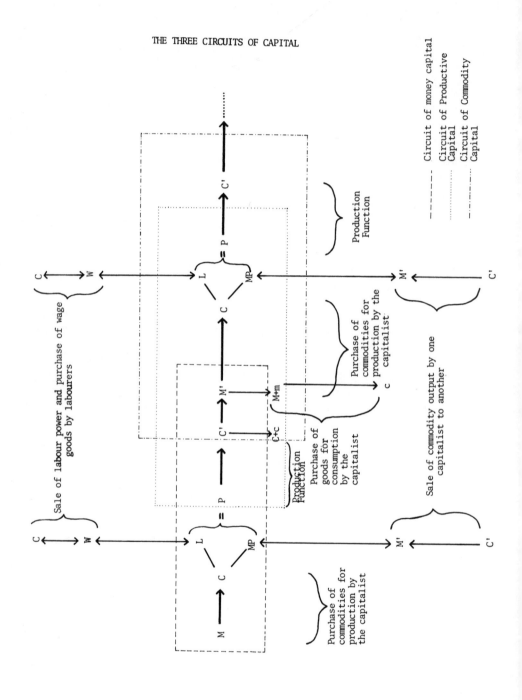

M	Money, also money capital.
M'	Money, also money capital.
m	Money, the difference between M' and M.
C	Commodity, usually commodity inputs.
C'	Commodity, usually output commodity; also called commodity capital.
L	Labour; labour power as sold by the labourer and labour as expended during production.
MP	Materials of production.
L and MP	together comprise C, which is the same as
P	Productive capital.
c	The difference between C' and C.
C	Constant capital.
V	Variable capital.
S	Surplus value.
$r = S/V$	Rate of surplus value.
$g = C/C+V$	Organic composition of capital.
$\bar{p}$	(Value) rate of profit.
p	Rate of profit (ambiguous as to whether money or value).
ρ	(Money) rate of profit.
Y_1	The value of output of Department I
Y_2	The value of output of Department II
Y	Total value of output
P_1	Price of the commodity produced by Department I.
P_2	Price of the commodity produced by Department II.
P_3	Price of the commodity produced by Department III.
R	Total Profit

In general subscript i stands for the ith Department, hence c_1 is the true value of constant capital used in Department I.

These as well as some other less frequently used symbols are also explained at the appropriate point in the text.

Numbers enclosed in { } refer to the number of quotations from Marx which are listed at the end in a separate section.

INTRODUCTION

Marx and Marxian economic theory have always occupied an anomalous position in Economics. Most universities do not teach Marxian economics as a separate subject and many do not even mention Marx as an important economist. If he has any place in the Economics coursework it is as a minor Post-Ricardian figure in the History of Economic Thought.

There has, however, always been an unsatisfied demand from the students that more be taught about Marx and his economics. Every student upheaval brings an upsurge in this demand with insinuations that somehow the Establishment in Economics deliberately suppresses Marxian economics since it challenges its orthodoxy. Faced with such protests, economists in universities have several choices. They may, of course, refuse to let temporary shifts in taste affect their curricula. They may alternatively bow to consumers' sovereignty and arrange for one of themselves to teach a course in Marxian economics or Radical Political Economy. This may be done with a view to dissipating the demand by demonstrating how boring or mistaken much of Marx's writing is. Alternatively, one may say that a course in Marxian economics should be set up only as long as demands for other similar courses, e.g. the Economic Theory of Major Douglas, are also met.

If no course is taught, the student who still wishes to learn about Marx's economics has further choice open to him. He may read Marxists or he may read Economists on Marx. The Marxists, following the bad precedent set by Hyndman, usually start off with primitive economies and go through every stage of society in a descriptive fashion trying to 'prove' by citing authorities that labour is the source of all wealth and that the Marxian scheme is still a valid if not the only, truth. Few of them do any justice to the analytical rich-ness of Marx's thought. The economists whom students can read on Marx, in contrast to their more orthodox colleagues, think of Marx as a major, not a minor, Post-Ricardian. The latter group claims that Marx is important for having anticipated many of the recent developments in economics. Marx, they say, anticipated Walras, Keynes, von Neumann, Leontieff, National Income Analysis, Two Sector Growth Models, etc. They look at Marx, there-fore, through the filter of modern economics. The advent of each new theory in economics enables some-one to reinterpret Marx or hail him as having anticipated this new theory. Of course it is only after the new theory has been propounded that Marx seems to appear in this light, not before. Thus it was the publication of the *General Theory* which gave people a new way of reading Marx. Suddenly they were able to read Keynes in Marx. (The inter-section of the two sets, Marxists and Economists, is luckily non-empty; it consists, however, of only one element - Paul Sweezy. His *Theory of Capitalist Development* is of course indispensable for anyone who wants to study Marx. It was published more than thirty years ago, however. There have been many developments in both economic theory and the political climate which necessitate a fresh look at Marxian economic theory).

The trouble with the approach of these economists is that their evaluation of Marx is coloured by current fashions and the prevailing tech-niques of economics. Modern economics is the dominant paradigm in the light of which Marx is praised by them as a pioneer, etc. But then Cournot anticipated Marshall, and Malthus, among others, anticipated Keynes. Quesnay anticipated Marx and Leontieff. We do not, however, feel compelled to teach courses in Economics of Quesnay, Malthus or Cournot. Even Marshall, Edgeworth and Pigou do not rate a course for themselves. Why, then, Marx?

Marxian economics has to be taught, if at all, due to the continued political relevance of Marx's analysis. I do not mean by this his relevance for an analysis of Soviet and Eastern European economies or as a guide to the often mystical pronouncements of the leaders and the economic planners of those countries. Marxian economic theory is a tool for analysing capitalism and it is as such that it deserves to be studied. In this sense, Marxian economic theory must be studied as separate from the main tradition in economics. This tradition claims as its own Adam Smith, David Ricardo, John Stuart Mill, Stanley Jevons,

Leon Walras, Bohm-Bawerk, and in modern days Marshall, Keynes, von Neumann, Leontieff among others. An attempt to fit Marx into this scheme of ideas can succeed only by emasculating his system or by making his fellow travellers uncomfortable. It is as the pioneer of a separate tradition in Economics, deriving as well as breaking away from the Classical school, that Marx is important.

This does not reduce the problem of confronting Marx's ideas with modern economic theory or with the classical tradition. Many analytical techniques developed in recent years are powerful logical aids. But in treating Marx on his own grounds one is saved the error of confusing his concerns with those of Ricardo. One is also spared the ambitious task of mathematizing or marginalizing Marx. If only Marx had read Jevons or known calculus[1] one often hears. (Marx knew the calculus and while there is no record of his having read Jevons, for a person of his wide reading one can only suppose that he read Jevons at some stage between 1871, the date of publication of *Theory of Political Economy* and 1883, the year Marx died. It is a puzzling matter that at least as yet no written record of Marx's reading of Jevons or Walras is available). I have tried to resist re-writing Marx in such a fashion.

The principle thesis of this book is that Marx's value theory is different from Ricardo's as well as from the Neoclassical theory. The role of value theory in Marx's work is to bring out the influence of the class struggle in capitalism on the economic relationships of exchange. Thus it is a necessary feature of the Marxian model that we have value equations and price equations as two separate systems. What is visible at the surface is the system of exchange relationships, and price equations describe this system. Underlying the exchange relationships are relations of production where the class division becomes manifest. Value equations describe these relations. A transformation from values to prices and vice versa is essential for understanding the reality of class division beneath the phenomenon of equality and free exchange under law. If this concern is ignored then Marx's system becomes a variant of Ricardo's system, and so suffers from the same analytical problems as the latter.

This view also makes it clear that the labour theory of value in

Marx is not a theory of relative prices or a theory of resource allocation. Value is a social relationship and not just an old-fashioned name for (production) price. This does not mean, however, that Marx is treated uncritically in these pages. His failure to adhere to the value price distinction rigorously is seen as the source of his mistakes in solving the transformation problem. His failure to relate his arithmetical examples of extended reproduction to his theory of uneven development and crises elsewhere in his works was pointed out by Rosa Luxemburg. I extend that discussion further and relate it to the value-price distinction.

A problem one faces when discussing Marx is that our minds are made up regarding his work before we ever read a word written by him. Some of us know that his prophecies have been proved wrong, that revolutions have not taken place in the developed capitalist countries, that workers have not been impoverished and that prosperity rather than crisis prevails. Others are equally convinced that he and he alone told the truth and that doom is around the corner. Few of us read Marx. We read about him. But when he is read it is in the form of isolated quotations, cited by some author to prove his special case. Reading this book is therefore no substitute for reading *Capital* in all its three volumes. But in order that readers may look at Marx's words without interpolation by me, all quotations from *Capital* have been grouped together at the end. It is sincerely hoped that readers will read these quotations in conjunction with the text.

Chaper II underlines the difference between Marxian economics, classical economics and Neoclassical economics. In order to understand this, we need to inquire into Marx's view of the nature of exploitation. In this and the following Chapter, I paraphrase Marx's historical perspective as much as is necessary to understand his value theory. No attempt is made in these pages to amend Marx's view of history or to make an apologia for it. Chapter IV then completes the basic background to an understanding of the value concepts.

Chapter V describes the three circuits of capital as contained in Vol. II of *Capital*. This area is usually neglected in most treatments of Marx. The importance of monetary relations in Marx's model comes out clearly only when we look at the three circuits together.

With Chapter VI and VII we are on the more familiar territory of
Marx's basic equations. I hope that readers have been sufficiently
warned by the material in the earlier chapters that these symbols and
equations are not to be manipulated mechanically. The historical
background should always be kept in mind.

The next five chapters form a discussion of the famous Transformation Problem. After a brief and perhaps to the scholars a sketchy
introduction, I outline Marx's solution and point out his mistakes.
The solution suggested by Bortkeiwicz is then outlined and in the light
of his solution, Marx's mistakes are clarified. The social content of
Bortkeiwicz's proposed solution differs from that of Marx and I
briefly discuss this. Chapter XI gives my view of why the Transformation
Problem needs to be solved in Marx's model. Since my view differs
considerably from prevailing interpretations, I examine the discussion
of Marx's model by Samuelson and Morishima. I also briefly discuss
Sraffa's work which has excited much interest among those interested
in Marxian economics.

The next four chapters outline Marx's model of Extended Reproduction. The basic model from the concluding chapters of Vol. II of
Capital is outlined in Chapter XIII. Rosa Luxemburg's critique of
Marx's model and her solution are then discussed. I have only taken
those aspects of her account which are of analytical interest. Even
her critique of Marx fails to bring out the relevance of value price
distinction and I suggest some tentative ways of integrating this
into the model in Chapter XVI.

One frequent criticism of Marxian theory is that its predictions
are not testable or that they have been tested and rejected but that
Marxists refuse to admit this. I have not gone into this methodology
question at all. Much of the argument here is conducted in what can be
called naive falsificationist approach.[1] I have analysed in some
detail the prediction about the falling rate of profit. Joseph
Gillman's empirical investigation of the law is summarised in Chapter
XVIII and I discuss the problem of specifying Marx's predictions in a
way that a proper test can be carried out.

In the last chapter, a number of topics are discussed concerning
the contemporary relevance of Marxian economic theory. Here again the

emphasis is on analytical aspects that arise in the further development of Marxian theory. This is not, however, a book on radical political economy and therefore I do not discuss racism, sexism, imperialism, etc. This is also not a critique of Neoclassical economic theory and therefore issues such as the recent debate on capital theory are ignored. This book treats Marxian economics as an ongoing research programme where many unsettled questions remain to be answered.[2] In order to keep the discussion accessible to as many people as possible, I have made it non-mathematical. By the same token, I have avoided the jargon of philosophers who write in this area.

THE ROLE OF VALUE THEORY IN CLASSICAL, NEOCLASSICAL AND MARXIAN
  ECONOMICS

A theory of value is at the heart of every major school of
economic thought. The notion of value is in itself philosophical but
a logically satisfactory value theory is crucial not only for tackling
theoretical problems but for answering practical and operational
questions as well. We begin with an attempt to understand the
differences in the role value theory plays in Marxian as against Neoclassical and Classical economics. By Classical economics we mean
the tradition of Adam Smith, David Ricardo and John Stuart Mill. Neoclassical economics is the dominant tradition today, pioneered by
William Stanley Jevons, Carl Menger and Leon Walras in the 1870's.

In modern (Neoclassical) economic theory, the role of value
theory is to provide a theory of relative prices. The simultaneous
determination of relative prices of all goods (except the numeraire)
and of the quantities produced and exchanged is the central problem
of the existence of general equilibrium. A major achievement of
recent developments in mathematical economics has been the fashioning
of an apparatus which with minimal assumptions about the nature of
consumer preferences and technology can prove the existence of an
equilibrium set of prices and quantities.[1]

In Classical economics, by contrast, value theory had a different
role. Its first task was to counter the Mercantilist fallacy of
regarding only precious metals (treasure) as valuable by showing that
wealth consisted of useful goods. But not all goods which had use
value commanded exchange value. Exchange values were determined not
so much by the ratio of a commodity to precious metals (its money price)

but the relative difficulty of producing that commodity. To simplify matters appropriately for an era before the advent of large scale factory production, the labour expended seemed to be the best determinant of relative values. Wealth consisted of valuable goods, goods which could be made by labour available in conjunction with other goods (machinery) which were also products of current or previous labour.

The rate of accumulation of wealth then depended on whether the recipients of income spent their wealth on producing more goods or on other and therefore non-productive uses. The final task of value theory was to tie together the questions of who received income and how they were likely to spend it to bring out the interdependent nature of value, accumulation and distribution.[2] In the Classical labour theory of value, prices of all goods are sought to be derived from the current labour input and the labour input embodied in materials of production. There was in the Classical tradition always some ambiguity as to whether labour was being used solely as a *measure* of value or whether it was being asserted that labour alone was the cause, the source of value. Much depended on which of these two possibilities was being asserted since from the view that labour is the sole source of value, a view adopted by many English radicals in the 1820's and 1830's, profits could be thought of as an unjust deduction from value created by labour alone. But even taking labour as a measure of value, many logical difficulties remain with the Classical labour theory of value.

A major problem is that the measure of value is not invariant with respect to the structure of production and the distribution of income. As an economy grows, changes in technology, in the amounts and varieties of goods produced and in the pattern of consumption, whether due to the growth of income or to changes in tastes, alter the value of a unit of labour. In order to avoid this problem one has to assume a rigidly fixed subsistence wage and an unchanged technology. If allowance is to be made for growth and technical change, these have to be specified as occurring in such a way that the value of labour remains unchanged. The exercise at this stage becomes unrealistic and tautological.[3]

Recent developments in mathematical economics and, in particular, the work of Leontieff, von Neumann and Sraffa have clarified many of the issues regarding the Classical labour theory of value.[4] The first issue is whether relative prices are proportional to the ratio of labour content alone. We now know that in as much as direct as well as indirect labour is used in the production of any commodity, indirect labour being embodied in the commodity inputs, we have to weight the indirect inputs by the rate of profit. Thus, we need information on the technology of labour and commodity inputs as well as the rate of profit prevailing in the economy, in order to derive relative prices. If in addition durable capital goods are used in the production process the calculus of labour theory is further complicated. But all these problems can now be analytically solved and an equilibrium vector of prices and quantities can be derived given the technical coefficients and the rate of profit. The Classical labour theory of value as reformulated in modern mathematical economics gives many insights into certain problems of economic theory such as valuation of capital and brings out the dependence of prices on the distribution of income.

The role of value theory in Classical and Neoclassical economics is to provide an explanation of the structure of observed prices and quantities. The differences in the approaches concern their emphasis on the static resource allocation problem as against a growth theoretic orientation. They are, however, confined to studying strictly economic relationships and aim to explain observed economic facts concerning quantities of different commodities including labour produced and consumed, prices charged for them, the rate of accumulation and of technical change, etc.

Marxian Value Theory

For Marx, value theory was a key to explaining the nature of capitalist society. The notion of value for him was central to an explanation of the prevailing social and economic conditions - of growing productive powers and wealth accumulation, of a class division of society into those who had to work for a living and those for whom they worked, of the contrast of poverty and riches. But value calculus for Marx was specific to a capitalist society. Unlike Neoclassical economic theory which extends its model to cover all possible societies through time and space, Marxian theory emphasises the historical relativity of economic categories. Thus for Marx value relationships are not valid for feudal or communist societies, only for a capitalist society. It is absolutely essential that Marx's notion of value be understood and contrasted with the similar-looking Classical theory of value. Extreme confusion and much futile debate has resulted from a failure to do so.

Value for Marx is a *social relationship*. The best way to understand this notion of value is to see how Marx deals with the problem of exploitation. A premise of the French Revolution and other parallel liberal democratic revolutions is the end of feudal privilege and of serfdom, the establishment of equality, freedom of contract and the ownership of private property without arbitrary hindrance. In a society where everybody is equal in the eyes of the law, and people freely enter into contract without coercion or compulsion, how can there be exploitation? It is this question that for Marx value theory sets out to answer first.

The first idea to get out of the way here is the notion of exploitation based on ignorance on the part of the exploited or due to imperfections in competitive structure. Following Joan Robinson [5] exploitation is defined in modern economics as the gap between wage and the Marginal product of labour due to monopoly elements. The notion of exploitation in Marx does not depend on such imperfections. The important task is to explain exploitation in a world free of such imperfections however real they may be.

Exchange is mutually beneficial in a world where exchange is based on freedom of contract {1I}. In capitalist societies, labourers are free to hire themselves out to the highest paying employer and employers are similarly free. These conditions are not universal in time and space but arise as a specific historical condition under capitalism. In a feudal society, a serf is not free to enter into contract with his lord nor with anyone else. At the level of free exchange and mutually beneficial trade, one cannot explain exploitation. If we confine ourselves to studying exchange relationships - at the level of economic *forms* as Marx would say - it is impossible to observe and/or explain exploitation {21}. To do this, we must go to production relationships or, as Marx would put it, to the realities behind the forms. For Marx, bourgeois political economy of his days was at fault because it studied economic problems only at the formal level of market exchange.

Relations of Production

What are the relationships of production? As all concepts and categories in Marx, these arise historically and are specific to certain societies or *modes of production*. One is now speaking of relationships of production specific to capitalism and the capitalist mode of production (and, one may add, a 19th century capitalism as Marx saw it). How for example are the relationships of production different in capitalist as against feudal society or in a subsistence economy? Let us begin with capitalism referring to other modes only as background.

In capitalism, first you have the category of *free labour* {16}. This free labour is free in two senses. It is free from feudal ties and any extra-economic compulsions: it is free to enter into contract. It is also free in another sense. It has been divested of its means of production. Unlike a farmer tilling his (owned or rented) land or a weaver with his loom working either for himself or in a putting out system, the free labourer has no means of production, no tools of trade to work with. This severing of means of production from labour is the outcome of a long historical process which renders peasants into unskilled industrial labour and breaks up Guilds and ruins cottage industries {17}. Capitalism sees the emergence of free labour which has no other way of sustaining itself except to find some machinery to work with, machinery owned by the capitalist. In a model of pure capitalism, you have only free labour and capitalists. In the real world, there are intermediate categories of self-employed, pro-fessionals, owner-cultivators, etc. The bulk of the population falls, however, in the free labour category.

11

The emergence of free labour may take different historical forms in different societies. In the United States, for example, except for the slavery in the southern states, much of the country had no feudal institutions and plenty of available land on which the individual farmer-cultivator could settle. The availability of uncultivated land provided an alternative outlet for the large waves of immigrants from Europe who formed the labour force in the industrial areas. These immigrants had often left a near-feudal peasant status and taken up the status of free labour in the U.S. The degree of exploitation in such a situation would be mediated by the availability of land on which a person could produce for himself.[6] By contrast, the emergence of free labour in many other countries takes the form of dispossessing of peasants or share croppers by some form of land reform legislation or by processes now known as detribalization-urbanization, migration to foreign plantations, etc.

In the U.K., the classic pattern was the Enclosure movement and the breakdown of cottage industries which dispossessed farmers and craftsmen and created over a period of two or three hundred years an industrial proletariat.[7] In many countries where introduction to capitalism has not immediately led to industrialization, we may have pools of landless labourers in a relation of feudal dependence or on permanent employment to the local landlord only slowly emerging as casual labour being paid money wages and free of the dependent status. The attainment of status of free labour is a progressive step in terms of elimination of social coercion but often it may lead to a worsening economic position. Often one encounters nostalgia for the days of 'benevolent landlords' who took paternal care of their labourers who upon migration are often worse off. It is important when analysing the economic situation in any particular country or age to know the historical form taken by the emergence of free labour or the proletaria

On the obverse side of the emergence of free labour is the con-solidation of class monopoly of means of production in the hands of the capitalists. This is once again an historical phenomenon, taking different particular forms in different societies but also revealing uniformities. First, it is a class monopoly not individual monopoly. A class monopoly of means of production is consistent with and, indeed, appears as competition among individual entrepreneurs. The class in whose hands the means of production concentrate is frequently called the Bourgeoisie but this word may also denote other elements - professionals, upper echelons of state bureaucracy, higher clergy, etc.[9] We shall therefore refer to the monopoly class as the class of capitalists.

The consolidation of means of production in the hands of the capitalists takes place at the expense of the feudal class on the one hand and many self-employed artisans, craftsmen at the other end. A struggle between the feudal and capitalist elements is a major feature of 18th and 19th century history of many European countries and while the outcome in most countries which are called developed today was in favour of the capitalists, it took different forms. The agitation regarding the abolition of Corn Laws and in favour of Free Trade was the classical platform of the struggle between feudal landlords and industrial capital in England (and like all such classical events is partly mythological). In other countries, the feudal landlords transformed themselves into industrial capitalists often with state aid (as in Japan after the Meiji Restoration) and even in England the feudal elements are not entirely absent from the capitalist class to this day. The American Civil War is another example (once again rather simplified) of a confrontation between industrial capitalism of the North and the feudal South. Another element is the transformation of commercial and merchant capitalists into industrial capitalists. This transformation is facilitated by a variety of institutional and legal forms, e.g. financial institutions such as Land Banks or State Industrial Banks, reforms involving confiscation of foreign capital or land-holdings. In different countries, particular events have dictated the combination of these various forms which have led to the concentration of means of production in the hands of the capitalists.[10]

It needs to be kept in mind constantly that while a model of capitalism with two antagonistic classes is at the heart of Marxian economics, in any particular historical (concrete) situation, one has to take into account many classes.[11]

The task of value theory is to explain why and how these relations of production lead to explotation. We have a contradiction in the Hegelian sense here between the emergence of free labour and its exploitation, between the breakdown of all artificial barriers to competition and the emergence of a class monopoly of means of production. The importance of value theory for Marx is that it makes the exploitation behind exchange *visible*; while price theory or value theory in Neoclassical economics analyses exchange, and relationships defined by exchange, the task of a value theory for Marx was to unmask explotation. The visible relationship between the employer and the worker is a commodity relationship {59}. We have, in the sense of Neoclassical economic theory, commodity markets everywhere and the labour market is only a particular example of a commodity market. The price of labour power (the commodity that the labourer supplies) is determined by supply and demand like the price of any other commodity. But unlike other commodities used during the production process, where the buyer as well as the seller is a capitalist, in the exchange of labour power (L) for money (M), we have a transaction taking place between two people belonging to two classes of society - the class of labourers dispossessed of the means of production and the class of capitalists, who own the means {60}. This class relation is hidden by the commodity relationship which takes place on an apparent basis of equality. The labourers appear as the commodity labour power and in selling labour power they seek to gain access to another commodity - a sum of money advanced - capital which is in its turn the form in which the capitalist appears in the market. In each case, men come into relationship with each other through the commodities they represent. This transformation of a social relationship, a class relationship into a commodity relationship, a relationship of exchange is what Marx calls *commodity fetishism*. Fetishism is peculiar to capitalism {3} {4}.

To understand this, let us look at feudalism. The relationship of the serf to the master is an openly exploitive social relationship {7}. The serf has to spend some part of his working days or some days

in the week working for the lord. The lord thus directly appropriates
a portion of the serf's labour for his own output. The serf's unfree
position makes his exploitation directly visible. In capitalism, not
only is the labourer free but a form of specialization (the commodity
mode of production) characterizes it {8} {2}. In earlier societies,
people produced partly for their own consumption and partly for exchange
in the market to buy other commodities. The producer appears on the
market with the fruits of his labour. In capitalism, production is
not for use but for exchange. The worker does not bring his product
on the market for exchange. He brings his labour power, he exchanges
it for a sum of money or a basket of goods but this is independent of
whichever commodity he is engaged in producing. He is not directly
involved with the end product of his work and in this sense he is
'alienated' from his productive activity. But the only way he can
live is by working (since he has no means of production at his disposal) and thus his 'free' status leads to his being transformed into
labour power {15}. His productive activity, essential for his
existence, is alienated from its end product. Labour power is purchased
and transformed into a final product which is exchanged against other
final products which are also transformed versions of labour power of
other workers. Thus workers relate to each other and to the capitalist
only through the mediation of commodities.

The productivity of labour power keeps the labourer alive and
perpetuates his 'free' status {44}. Similarly the productivity of
machinery legitimises the surplus the capitalist appropriates. The
productivity of the thing perpetuates the status of the human beings
corresponding to the thing. The capitalist gets the surplus because
of the historically given social relationship of private property
and the circumstances of the class monopoly of means of production. At
the level of exchange, the productivity of capital, e.g. machinery,
buildings, etc., appears as the productivity or usefulness of the
capitalist. (In other social relationships, machines can be productive
but the surplus need not go to a capitalist class since such a class
may not exist). Since social relationships appear as commodity
relationships we have commodity fetishism {4}. Commodity relationships
tend to be seen as ahistorical and timeless. One is led to regard

15

exchange relationships as timeless and the calculus of economic theory as being applicable to all states of society. You can visualise the feudal lord as 'optimising' in the same sense as an economic firm or entrepreneur. At the level of exchange this appears to be so and is legitimate, but the nature of exploitative relationships is different for feudal and capitalist systems.

The contradiction between the juridically free status of the labourer and his exploitation is the *original* contradiction of capitalism. It is original since it appears at the origin in capitalism {2}. In no other society does exploitation take the value form since in no society does it have to be masked from visible relationships. The commodity form of labour power confronting the commodity form of capital is a peculiarly capitalist event. In some societies (e.g. the USSR), the legal form of property ownership may change and take such forms as state ownership of all or some means of production, but the original contradiction remains in as much as the labourer has to sell himself for living, that he is alienated from his production process, that he confronts a ruling class in a commodity form.[13]

III

UNDIFFERENTIATED AND ABSTRACT LABOUR: AN ABSTRACTION AND AN HISTORICAL PROCESS

We have been using the words product and commodity interchangeably, but for Marx this is an important distinction. All economies produce *products*, only in capitalism do products take the form of *commodities* { 2 }. Commodities are produced mainly, if not entirely, for exchange. Products as well as commodities have use value but commodities need exchange value. In a subsistence economy, producers produce for own consumption. In capitalism, all production is for exchange.

Duality of Specific Labour and Abstract Labour

This is a very important distinction -- the dual value form as Marx called it { 5 }. It is hardly novel since economists before Marx and since have known of the distinction between use value and exchange value (though they did not draw the distinction between products and commodities). For Marx, the commodity mode of production and the dual value form became a determining social phenomenon in the following sense. Products embody different kinds of labour, specific labour of a tailor or carpenter or a joiner. When they are exchanged as commodities, relative value ratios are established which make these separate products freely transformable into one another. A coat becomes a table which becomes a machine since they all exchange at determinate ratios. The specific labour (and workmanship) of a joiner or a tailor is stripped away and ratios are determined in relation to the abstract or undifferentiated labour { 3 }.

At one stage this is a formula - the basic formula of labour theory of value. What determines the ratio is the amount of socially necessary labour time required to produce a commodity relative to another {1}. This is quite a standard definition in classical labour theory. For Marx, what is important is that this reduction of all products to a general value formula hides behind it a specific historical process. The reason why specific labour can be reduced at a common measure - to abstract labour more efficiently under capitalism - under the commodity mode of production rather than under any previous mode - is the simultaneous disappearance of skilled specialised labour. The historical process is that which converts craftsmen, artisans and specific skilled workers into the proletariat, divorced from their means of production, free of Guild regulations. The process of division of labour reduces a particular man to a particular operation. The element of skill is reduced to the element of common, homogeneous, undifferentiated labour. This is a long historical process and never fully achieved. There are hand-made goods by skilled craftsmen in developed economies today but the overwhelming bulk of commodities can be exchanged against each other without reference to the specific labour they embody.

The labour value ratio is therefore simultaneously a formula and a historical process. This is why the category of abstract, undifferentiated labour is not an abstraction but an historical tendency.[1] Upon reduction to undifferentiated labour, the only thing that commonly characterises specific types of labour is that it is *human* labour. There is no other distinction whether of skill, location, caste or tribe. The general exchange formula - by virtue of the fact that all products exchange on the market - bares the common element in different working situations and thus combines the individual workers into a class of proletariat.

The special feature of capitalism - of the commodity mode of production - is not so much that production is for exchange, since in many pre-capitalist economies extensive internal as well as external trade often existed. The emergence of a commodity market in labour is for Marx the special feature distinguishing capitalism from previous modes of production. The market for labour is different from all other commodity markets and this difference has to be understood if we are to distinguish Marx from, say, Ricardo. Marx introduces the distinction between labour and labour power {14}. The agreement to sell labour is a recurring agreement, daily, weekly or annually re-entered into. In order to be free to re-contract at the end of the day, the labourer must preserve his freedom. He cannot make a life-long contract - that is akin to slavery. What, in fact, the labourer sells everyday is, according to Marx, labour power - the potential capacity to work for a given length of working day {15}. In order that he can do this again and again, he must be able to reproduce himself - not reproduction in the sense of population growth but in the sense of keeping alive and preserving his capacity for work. The value of labour power - the commodity the labourer sells - is determined like the value of any other commodity by the social labour necessary for its reproduction - the subsistence basket taking into account historical as well as moral considerations {19}. The value of labour power is the same for all labourers since all labours are interchangeable and have been reduced to abstract, undifferentiated labour by the historical process referred to above. The value of labour power according to Marx is decided *independently of and prior to* the specific job that the labourer might be engaged on. Once he has sold labour power (L) in exchange for a sum of money (M) to obtain a certain basket of goods, the labourer's time for the length of the working day is at the disposal of the capitalist. The gap between exchange value of labour power and its use value now becomes important. What the labourer expends during the working day is no longer labour power - no longer the potential capacity but actual labour. The use value of labour when employed by the capitalist along with the materials of production (MP) is the value added by the worker {20}. This use value of labour is in excess of the exchange value of labour power. This gap is the surplus value and the capitalist seeks to buy labour because he expects to reap surplus value {22}.

The gap between the exchange value and use value of labour, the notion that under capitalism what the labourer sells is labour power and the determination of the exchange value of labour power independent of the specific job the labourer engages in - these three elements are crucial to Marxian Labour theory. In each case we must bear in mind that for Marx the class relation is crucial in the labour market; indeed it is unique to it since other commodities are exchanged by buyers and sellers who are formally as well as actually on an equal footing. The exchange relationship and the form that the transaction - the sale of labour - takes is embodied in the wage form. Neither the worker nor the capitalist directly perceives the division between the value of labour power and surplus labour. The worker sees himself being paid for the full day's work though only a part of that day is equivalent to the value of the labour power he sells.

Marx clearly is concerned here with unskilled labour or labour of that level of skill which can form a common denominator, and interchangeable mass. But it is very important not to interpret the Marxian model mechanically. Thus many critics and defenders of Marx have equated the value of labour power with the wage rate and insisted that a rigid subsistence real wage rate is an essential element of Marx's model. Marx himself mentions in one instance that the value of labour power forms a floor below which the wage does not fall {35}. Indeed the determination of the wage rate or of the gap between the real wage and the value of labour power is a relatively unexplored area in Marxian economics. The partisans of Marx insisted on the tendency towards a subsistence wage as an indictment of capitalism, whereas for Marx's critics a subsistence wage represented an assumption at the same time necessary for the model and obviously falsified by empirical trends. We must, however, bear in mind that for Marx class relations are crucial to the course of the labour market and the dynamics of class relations must be recognised as an important factor in the Marxian model. Real wages can rise with accumulation in the Marxian model {48}. What is important to bear in mind is that the true course of real wages, whether upward or downward, is not automatic nor does it depend mechanically on rising productivity of labour. It is the workers' struggle as a class against the capitalists as a class - a struggle which witnesses growth of Unions, strikes, lockouts, legislation, political action, etc., - which is the important moving force in determining the course of real wages. The importance of class struggle is specifically mentioned by Marx in the context of forces determining the length of the working day {25} {27}. His rejection of any mechanical rule such as a wage fund doctrine and emphasis on worker's struggle is brought out in his occasional writings.[2]

The Creation of Surplus Value and the Role of Money

We have already quoted Marx as saying that exchange cannot create surplus value nor can one observe exploitation at the level of exchange. It is essential for our purpose to understand the process of creation of surplus value for this is the explanation and measure of exploitation. Since exchange cannot create surplus value, it cannot be through an analysis of exchange value that we can explain exploitation. Thus, given the dual value form, it must be use-value. We seek an explanation of exploitation in use-value.

In modes of production previous to the commodity mode, products are exchanged for money and then money is converted back into products. the producer appears on the market with products, not with money.[3] Indeed, the only role of money in this situation is to facilitate and generalize the two-person form of barter. If this happened in a commodity mode, we could describe this exchange cycle as Commodity-Money-Commodity or C - M - C. The commodity mode is, however, distinguishable by the fact that production is for exchange and not for use. The capitalist appears on the market with money (M), buys raw materials, rents machines and buys labour power (C) and sells the final product at a profit (M'). M' is larger than M. Indeed, there would be no sense in having a commodity form if at the end of the production process profit was not made by the capitalists. We have then the cycle M - C · M'. How is it that M' > M; what explains the money profit made by the capitalist?

The clue for Marx is the initial stage where the capitalists buy commodities, i.e. factors of production, with money. There are three components here - raw materials, labour power and machinery. In buying raw materials since they are bought from other capitalists (excluding for the time being such circumstances as a peasant sector or a colony from which these may be bought), except for incidental swindling and cheating, the full value for a raw material must be paid. This is uncontroversial and is indeed the definition of value added. It is more important to understand why Marx says that machines do not create surplus value. Marx does not deny that machines are productive i.e. that they have value. The value produced by a machine during the productive process is equated to the rental paid by the capitalist for the use of the machine. Whether the capitalist owns the machine or rents it is irrelevant here for the economic calculation. The point is that the value produced by the machine - the value transferred from the machine to the final product as Marx would put it - is exactly matched by the flow price of the machine. This means that the cost of the machine and the cost of the raw materials are already included in the initial sum of money advanced, M. It is the third element purchased with M - labour power which is then left as the only possible source of *surplus value* - value over and above that incorporated in the purchase price {13}.

Labour creates surplus value by virtue of the fact that the unequal class relation operating in the market for labour creates a gap between its use value and exchange value {22}. Of the three factors of production, machines and raw materials are bought and sold by capitalists and hence there is no possibility of surplus value being extracted. Such incidental cheating or underpricing that may occur only affects the distribution of surplus value within the class of capitalists. Labour is the one commodity which is sold by the worker and bought by the capitalist {60}. It is the productivity of labour, productivity of value and of surplus value, which creates the demand for labour on the part of the capitalist {20}.

We have come to the significant divide between Marxian economic theory and all other schools of economics - Classical, Neoclassical and Keynesian. The frequent misunderstanding concerning Marxian theory and especially the confusion between Marxian and Ricardian theory stems from the seemingly identical labour theory of value used by both Marx and Ricardo. Ricardo begins by taking as given the existence of three classes of income receivers and his concern is with the effect of accumulation on the shares received by the three classes. The Ricardian theory of value is thus also a theory of distribution in a growing economy. As a part of this theory, prices are sought to be reduced to current and dated labour inputs. It has now been shown conclusively by many people that if fixed capital is used in the production process, a rate of profit must be included in a price calculation.[4] Marx's concern is not so much with the determination of prices. He is perfectly aware that from the viewpoint of the capitalist (and of political economy) one can have a cost of production theory of prices {80}{81}. In this case, profits are a difference between price and unit costs and different explanations - abstinence, entrepreneurship, risk bearing, etc. - can be advanced for this difference. Marx is interested in the relation between prices and values since this alone can explain profits as being generated by surplus value. Only value theory shows for Marx that cost-based prices are disguising the social relations of value.

For Marxian theory it is *surplus value that is created by labour.*. All commodities have value. Machines are productive and so is labour. In the case of labour alone, due to the unequal nature of social relations, there is a gap between use-value and exchange value of labour power. At the end of each productive process the labourer reproduces himself and the capitalist *accumulates* wealth {44}. This asymmetry of result is due to the asymmetry of class relation. Under conditions of exchange, such an asymmetry cannot be derived directly from the initial conditions of equality. Divorced from this class context, the Marxian theory is indistinguishable from Ricardian theory. The difference lies not in the characterization of the productive process, similar for all schools of economics, but in the process of buying and selling labour power which lies at the beginning of the productive process and leads to appropriation of surplus value by one class. Throughout, all the participants perceive only legitimate exchange relations and not unequal relations of class and exploitation.

Given any theory of price formation which is consistent and satisfies the usual requirement of equality of rate of profits in different indus-- tries, our task is to link value relations (also consistent within themselves) to price relations. We need to make value relationships explicit and outline their logical structure. Then we go on to discuss the transition - the transformation - of value relations into price relations.

IV

CREATION OF SURPLUS VALUE AS A SOCIAL PROCESS

We return to the problem of creation of surplus value and now
we can see it as a social process. Marx analyses in some detail the
process of production and makes at this stage a distinction between
the physical process of production and the value process of production.
The physical process of production combines the services of the
machine, the raw materials and the specific skills of labour to
produce output {63}. This is the familiar production function of
economic theory. The value process of production has to do with the
buying of inputs and the selling of output (at which stage it becomes
a commodity) in the market thus dissolving the specific characteristics (use value) of whatever is produced by reducing it to its
exchange value freely translatable into another commodity. The
useful specific skills of labour embody the specific values of machinery
and raw materials along with its own value into the final output.

The physical process of production - 'the production of commodities by means of commodities' (including labour power) is similar in
different modes of production. Surplus value is specific to capitalism in the sense that while the production process may generate a
surplus it takes a value form only in capitalism and belongs to the
owner of money capital only in capitalism. The capitalist comes on
the market with a sum of money (M) but it is only when he *advances* it
by buying means of production and raw materials (MP) as well as labour
power (L) that the sum of money functions as *capital*. In buying
these various inputs, he converts money capital into *productive
capital* (P). We have then here half a cycle:

$$M \rightarrow C \diagdown^{L}_{MP} \} \; = \; P$$

This notation for the M - M' cycle was employed by Marx. In advancing a sum of money (M) the capitalist buys commodity inputs (C). The commodity inputs (C) comprise of labour (L) and material of production (MP). Together (L) and (MP) become productive capital (P) in the hands of the capitalists. Thus the first half of the M - M' cycle is the conversion of a sum of money into money capital (by advancing it) and purchasing productive capital with it.

The production process then converts C into another commodity whose amount is indicated by C'. This is the output of the process but the capitalist is not interested in C' until it is converted again into money. C' is thus output in the form of *commodity capital* When he sells C' for a sum of money M' then the circuit is completed. The other half cycle is P → C' → M'. Temporary or cyclical shrinkage of the market and the general problems of marketing affect the price at which C' can be converted to M'. In general M' > M and C' > C. The difference (M' - M) belongs to the capitalist because it appears that by virtue of his ownership of M, P belongs to him and therefore whatever is produced by P over and above 'costs of production' belongs to him. The physical process of production is thus seen as a function of the capitalist. It is not, however, his ownership of machinery that entitles him to the surplus. Whether he owns or rents machinery is irrelevant; he will still pocket the difference between M' and M. The machinery is his *property* (when he owns it) whether it is idle or in use. The labour power becomes his property only during use - during the length of the working day {64}. By itself machinery cannot produce anything; by himself, without access to means of production, the worker cannot live. From the worker's point of view he is exchanging his commodity - labour power - for a sum of money to obtain a bundle of commodities for subsistence. He sees the process as C → M → C. The capitalist needs to purchase labour power and machinery to produce C' but he is only interested in C' as a temporary abode of exchange value. He will sell it for M' and recover profits.

The value process of production is thus larger than the physical process since it includes the latter as a stage. This needs to be emphasised here since it will become a crucial distinction when we come to a discussion of the transformation problem. Surplus value is created by the use value property of labour power. The process of buying inputs and selling outputs - entrepreneurship, risk bearing, etc. - is a function of the owner of money capital. The capitalist can convert money capital into productive capital only because due to historical circumstances labour power - the commodity sold by the 'free' labourer - has become exchangeable {43}. Without this background and viewed purely as an exchange process, the exploitation of labour and creation of surplus value are not understandable. Surplus value is created in the process of production but appropriated and realized in money terms only as part of the value process. The participants in the whole process view it as a matter of exchange (and therefore price) relationships and not in terms of value relationships. At the level of exchange, profits are the difference between money value of output (M') and the money costs of production (M). Profit thus appears as a legitimate category whereas surplus value is a category based on exploitation. *It is the task of the labour theory of value, the task of political economy as Marx sees it, to explain the social process by which exploitation is 'dissolved', as it were, at the level of exchange and profits emerge at the visible level from an underlying unobservable surplus value relationship.* It is this problem that we must next tackle. While its full resolution will be discussed in the context of the transformation problem, we set up the background to it in the next Chapter.

V

THE THREE CIRCUITS OF CAPITAL

We can set out in some detail three ways of looking at the value
and the physical processes of production following Marx's discussion
in Vol. II of *Capital*.[1] These three ways are called three circuits
of capital - the commodity capital (C' - C') circuit, the productive
capital (P - P) circuit and the money capital (M - M') circuit. The
three circuits of capital are put together in Chart I. In one sense,
it is of no consequence which place you start the circuit at as long
as you complete it. But as we have seen, the two former circuits
underplay the role of money as capital. They also obscure the social
relation by which the owner of money capital buys labour power. Also,
surplus value is prominent in the M - M' circuit and becomes the
driving force of economic activity whereas it is not apparent in the
other two circuits.

The device of circular flow of income to describe the inter-
dependence of consumption, production and exchanges is familiar in many
textbooks of economics.[2] The circuits described below are similar to
circular flow except that while circular flows describe static conditions, the circuits portray a dynamic process where accumulation
and growth in real and money quantities are taking place {74}. But
even within the three circuits, as we mentioned above, the circuit of
money capital brings out the role of class relations in value theory
more clearly than the other two circuits. Many of the modern
approaches to Marx's value theory ignore the money capital circuit
and hence minimize the difference between Marxian and other approaches
to value theory.

The circuit of money capital is the most important in a commodity mode of production since production is undertaken not for use but for profit. The capitalist wants to have his profits not in terms of fina output but in terms of money. This is because he has originally advanced money capital (M) and he needs to recover his expenses and make profit in money terms. He is then free to reinvest money in the same industry, in another industry or to buy consumer goods. Thus the circuit of money capital begins with purchase of commodities which will form productive capital (P) in the hands of the capitalist. The circuit ends with the sale of output (C') and realisation of a money sum (M'). Exchange forms the beginning and the end of the process. Money lying as a hoard or spent directly on use values (consumer goods) is not capital since it only performs its function of being a medium of exchange. Money becomes capital for Marx only when it is advanced {56}. Capital has the property of being value which generate surplus value or of being self-expanding value {57}. This self ex-pansion takes place not at either end of the circuit which only in-volves exchange but in the middle where the commodities (inputs) bough are used as productive capital to produce a greater value of output in commodity terms (C') than was put in. The commodity composition of the output (C') is of course different from that of the inputs (C) for any one producer. What we call C breaks down into labour power (L and materials of production (MP); the latter again is many different commodities which form the inputs. The first part of the exchange M - C pre-supposes developed markets for L and MP as well as available supplies of them as and when needed.

The exchange M - L of money for labour power is the crucial social relation {60}. This is a simple commodity exchange of equiva-lents at the visible stage. The owner of M is also the owner of means of production and confronts the seller of labour power as not just any ordinary buyer of labour power (as would be the case with employ-- ment as a domestic servant or as a government functionary) but as a capitalist who wants him to join the production process to realise his capital. This exchange relationship is thus a class relationship since it is the labourer's separation from the means of production which makes labour power a commodity. Divorced from this class con-text, the M - L exchange would appear as a straightforward exchange of equivalents on a basis of equality. Divorced from this class context, it is hard to understand the role of exploitation.

The other part of the M - C exchange is the M - MP purchase. There is a difference that Marx emphasises between labour power and other commodity inputs. Markets for commodities pre-date the emergence of capitalism though they are fully developed only under capitalism. In this sense, commodity markets are no different under capitalism except that they are universal. It is the emergence of the labour market that differentiates capitalism. Another difference between labour power and other commodities can be seen from the point of view of the sellers of these commodities {64}. For the labourer, labour power is a commodity to be exchanged for money which will be in its turn spent on consumables C - M - C. For the seller of other commodities which become inputs, these commodities form commodity capital (C') emerging at the end of their productive process which they are now converting by sale into money (M') to either reinvest as capital in the productive process or spend as revenue on consumer goods. This is the reason why commodities other than labour power cannot be exploited; their surplus value is already realised by their sellers. In this sense, one can distinguish between the subjective (L) and the objective (MP) elements of productive capital. Labour power is a commodity in the hands of its seller but becomes capital in the hands of its buyer since he can use it to create surplus value. Other commodities (MP) are capital in the hands of the seller and capital in the hands of the buyer - commodity capital to be sold in the first case and productive capital to be used in the other case.

At the other end of the circuit, the output (C') is sold for money (M'), and as an abstraction one can think of the value of C' as being C (equal in value to the inputs) + c (surplus value embodied in output) although the composition of the initial C and the terminal C' are different. Similarly M' can be divided into M (equal to the original sum advanced) + m (surplus value in money form). As long as C' remains unsold it forms commodity capital, but the point is not to hoard it (except for speculation) but to sell it for a sum of money which will yield a profit. Having realised M', the end use can vary according to the individual capitalist. As a general form, we can say that in simple reproduction (i.e. no net accumulation), M is again advanced for C in the second round and m is spent on consumer goods by the capitalist. Until M' is spent it forms a hoard but becomes capital when advanced. M can of course be advanced in a different industry and in expanded reproduction m can also be advanced. Again m may be such a small quantity that many circuits have to be gone through before the sum of these amounts can be invested if there are indivisibilities in the inputs.

Although the crucial social relation manifests itself in M - L exchange, the production of surplus value is accomplished in the middle third of the circuit. This is the process of production which takes the commodity inputs (C) which comprise labour (L) and materials of production (MP) - together making up of productive capital (P) and generates output (C'). $C\genfrac{<}{}{0pt}{}{L}{MP}\} = P \to C'$. It is a purely technological relationship although the organisation of production changes as the technology changes. A 'putting out' system, whereby the capitalist advanced raw materials to workers to transform into output, and a factory system are different organisational forms (and these have their implications for the value relations which we shall not go into). The output C' need not be physical output; it can as well be services {66}.

Marx mentions that since the owner of M has purchased C, brought together L and MP, the production process seems a function of capital and hence of the capitalist.[3] The entrepreneur of later 19th century economic theory thus appears as a reflection of the ownership of M and the productive process which is a purely technological relationship becomes his function in capitalist production. The technology would be invariant under another mode of production - under socialism but the social relationship would be different. The apparent productivity of the entrepreneur is a by-product of the structure of property rights.

There is however a difference between capitalism and previous systems. Industrial capitalism not only concerns itself with appropriation of surplus value but also creation of surplus value. Thus it is not usuary, speculation or market restrictions that are important in this system but the production of surplus value. By constantly changing technology, the system aims to improve the productivity in the C → P → C' stage. Feudal exploitation exists on a static technology and does not create surplus value on the ever expanding scale of capitalism.[4]

The M - M' circuit can of course be interrupted at various stages. At the beginning, appropriate quantities of the commodities and labour power may not be available or the sum of money may not be advanced at all and may lie idle as a hoard. At the end there may be no possibility of selling all of C' or M' may be less than M. These matters are important in discussing crises but do not affect the discussion at this stage {65}.

The importance of the M - M' circuit is in the fact that it is most often forgotten that money is the starting and the end point of economic activity in capitalism. In the other two circuits, money appears as a mere intermediary and can be easily ignored. The function of money as money capital, i.e. more than just a medium of exchange, comes out only in this circuit.

The P - P circuit starts with productive capital and by transforming output (C') into inputs for the second stage, returns to P. We may call it Input-Output-Input circuit. We begin therefore with labour power and materials of production already in the hands of the capitalist though we do not ask how they came to be there. In a sense the factors of production are already in their employment at the start of a circuit. The function of money as capital is suppressed in this circuit since the exchange C' - M' - C can be easily seen to be an exchange of equivalents with money performing its role only as a medium of exchange. If we can assume that at the economy level it would be always possible to exchange C' for the requisite quantities of C, then the intermediation of money can be ignored altogether {70}.

We can regard the purpose of economic activity as consumption since the acquisition of consumer goods occurs in the circuit at least at two distinct points. Thus the worker exchanges labour power for a sum of money only to spend it on consumer goods. In Marx's notation, this is the L - M - C exchange. The capitalist on the other hand having realised M' at the end of the production process will spend the part he does not reinvest on consumption. Let us say

31

out of M', he reinvests M and spends m on consumption goods. In this case instead of C' - M' - C we have two circuits. One is the Output-Money-Input, C' - M - C, and the other is the circuit of surplus value in commodity form (c) converted into surplus value in money form (m) to be spent on consumption goods (c). We then have simple reproduction - no net accumulation since the same amount (C) is invested at the beginning of each period. The end purpose of economic activity from the point of view of the worker and the capitalist is then easily seen to be consumption, but such a view is misleading according to Marx {67}.

The P - P circuit does not explicitly bring out the crucial property of capital being a value producing surplus value. The difference between M - M' is clearly brought out in the money circuit. In the P - P circuit, the initial and terminal items may be different in composition and also in value. If labour productivity in particular and technology in general are changing constantly, as Marx emphasised, the end of the process is different and perhaps not directly comparable with the beginning. Surplus value thus disappears (or is obscured) in the P - P circuit.

The C' - C' circuit is similar (but not identical) to the P - P circuit in emphasising the commodity aspects of economic activity {72}. We start with surplus value already embodied in C' at the beginning and have then an Output-Input-Output circuit. Both P - P and C' - C' presume that all the other commodities which are inputs already exist in sufficient quantities. Marx describes Quesnay's *Tableau Economique* to be an example of C' - C' circuit {73}. In modern terms, the Leontieff Input-Output table or Sraffa's system of equations can be also seen as C' - C' circuit.[5] At an aggregate level, we sum the difference between C' (output) and C (input) for all sectors and obtain National Income. Now the c - m - c and the L - M - C components are described as consumers' expenditure and the rest as investment. Similarly, expressions can be derived for total income and output. The C' - C' circuit is thus the one we are most familiar with in modern economics {71}.

SIMPLE REPRODUCTION AND EXPANDED REPRODUCTION. A PRELIMINARY VIEW.

In the previous section, the discussion of circuits had to be carried out using the same notation for inputs as for output. We mentioned at some points that the commodity composition of C' was different from that of C. We could have also brought out the difference in the commodities purchased by capitalists in c - m - c exchange as against those purchased by workers in L- M - C exchange. We clearly need to disaggregate our circuits in many commodities. There is a second more important reason why we need to disaggregate. The role of prices and especially of differences in relative prices cannot be brought out in the general notation of the circuits. Even in a C' - C' circuit, while the capital function of money is ignored, the influence of relative prices can be brought out by disaggregation. Disaggregation of the value relations and the price relations will also be crucial in understanding the nature of the transformation problem.

Marx pioneered a two and three sector representation of economic activity. In one sense, his representation is an advance upon Quesnay's *Tableau* since his sectoral classifications are much more relevant to an industrial economy. Consumption and investment relations are linked with production and distribution. At this stage, we shall confine ourselves to a representation of a two and three sector model in *value terms* and we must always keep in mind that value categories are not directly observable in price relationships, e.g. in published data.

We have two sectors, or Departments as Marx called them. Department I produces the commodity which is used as constant capital - an investment good. Department II is the consumption good. For each Department we measure the value sums embodied in constant capital (C), variable capital (V) and surplus value (S). Total output in each Department we indicate by Y. We have

$$
\begin{array}{ll}
C_1 + V_1 + S_1 \;\vert=\; Y_1 & \text{Department I} \\
C_2 + V_2 + S_2 \;\vert=\; Y_2 & \text{Department II} \\
\hline
C \;+\; V \;+\; S \;\vert=\; Y &
\end{array}
\tag{1}
$$

In Department I, C_1 is the amount of value of constant capital used in Department I - its consumption of its own output. V_1 is the amount of variable capital - the value of labour power used in Department I. S_1 is the amount of surplus value. Thus in our previous notation we have the value of inputs (C) as $C_1 + V_1$ with C_1 standing for the value of MP and V_1 for value of L. Similarly for Department II, we have C_2 - the value of constant capital - output of Department I - used up in Department II and V_2 is the amount of its own output used up by Department II. In physical terms, Y_1 and Y_2 are different and so would be S_1 and S_2. The physical composition of C_1 and C_2 is the same as that of Y_1 and of V_1 and V_2 as that of Y_2. Note that the C in this chapter has a different meaning from that of C in the previous chapter. We have therefore used italics in this chapter to bring out the difference.

Having described the two department table, we can establish some functional relationships. We have implicitly indicated that the column and row sums are the same. Thus $C + V + S = Y_1 + Y_2 = Y$. In simple reproduction, the same value of total output is produced year after year - a system with zero growth rate. This clearly implies that the total output of Department I (Y_1) must not exceed the total usage of constant capital in the two Departments ($C_1 + C_2 = Y_1$). Thus we have a balancing equation, $Y_1 = C$. This together with the total identity implies that value of output of Department II (Y_2) must equal the total amount of variable capital (V) and surplus value (S). Thus, the output of Department II has to consist of wage goods as well as goods consumed by the capitalists. After replacing the amount of constant capital consumed in each period, the entire value is spent on the output of Department II.

In order to make a further distinction between wage-goods and other consumer goods, we add a third Department to our model. In particular we can make the distinction that the third Department absorbs surplus value while Department II produces only wage-goods. A three-Department scheme will be found useful in discussing many problems in Marxian theory as well as in analysing contemporary discussions about the nature of modern capitalism. We write down the three-Department scheme as follows:

$$
\begin{array}{ll}
C_1 + V_1 + S_1 \quad\big|\; = Y_1 & \text{Machine goods} \\
C_2 + V_2 + S_2 \quad\big|\; = Y_2 & \text{Wage goods} \qquad\qquad (2) \\
C_3 + V_3 + S_3 \quad\big|\; = Y_3 & \text{Other goods} \\
\hline
C \;+ V \;+ S \quad\big|\; = Y &
\end{array}
$$

Now there is a symmetry in a situation of simple reproduction between the column sums and the row sums. But there is a crucial difference. The output of Department III (Y_3) does not enter as input into the other two Departments, its only function is to absorb the surplus value created in the system. The role of Department III can be discussed in the context of the problem of *realization of surplus value*.

As we have said above, the capitalist has to sell his output in the market before he can realize surplus value (C' - M'). The schema above suffers from the drawback that it is not M - M' circuit but C' - C' circuit. We can still analyse the conditions under which the realization problem *does occur* i.e. the conditions of equilibrium in simple reproduction. In the two- Department schema (1) above the output of Department I (in value terms) which has to be sold outside the Department is ($Y_1 - C_1$), whereas the demand by Department II for the output of Department I is represented by C_2. The equality of C_2 and ($Y_1 - C_1$)[$C_2 = V_1 + S_1$] is reciprocated by the demand of Department I for the output of Department II [$V_1 + S_1$] and the output of Department II sold outside itself [$V_2 - (V_2 + S_2)$] . Notice, however, that the role of money is made subsidiary and can be entirely eliminated. Indeed, one can criticise Marx (as we shall see below Rosa Luxembourg

35

did) for emphasizing in Vol. II the importance of M - M' circuit and the qualitative difference it made compared to the C' - c' circuit for understanding the capitalist system while himself couching all his numerical examples in C - C' terms. In this way he emasculated the qualitative dynamics in the value system.

The three-Department schema is then just an elaboration of the previous one except that more inter-Departmental transactions have got to take place. *The more such transactions are required, the greater the uncertainty whether the surplus value would be automatically realized and therefore the greater the possibility of crises.* Let us see how this may happen. In the two Departmental model we have three transactions taking place. The capitalists of Department I have to pay the money equivalent of V_1 to purchase labour power which in turn will lead to labourers exchanging that money for a part of the output of Department II. Also the money equivalent of surplus value S_1 in Department I is spent buying goods from Department II. Such money is realized when Department II finds the money equivalent of C_2 to purchase that value of constant capital from Department I.

In the C - M - C notation of the previous chapters, the three transactions are:

(i) $\quad L_1 \ (= V_1) \rightarrow \ M_1 \ \rightarrow \alpha_1 Y_2$

(ii) $\quad S_1 \ \rightarrow m_1 \rightarrow \alpha_2 Y_2$

(iii) $\quad C_2 \ \rightarrow M_2 \rightarrow \alpha_3 Y_1$

In the above M_1, M and M_2 are sums of money, whereas V_1, S_1, C_2, Y_1 and Y_2 are values. By definition α_1, α_2 and α_3 are proportions lying between zero and unity. Intra-Departmental purchases can be deduced from the above three transactions.

Thus $V_2 + S_2$ equal $(1 - \alpha_1 - \alpha_2) \ Y_2$ and so on.

By comparison, the three-Department model entails six transactions between the Departments. In each case a portion of the Department's output has to be sold and the money used to purchase goods from the other Departments. If at any stage there is a tendency to hoard, or a temporary shrinkage of the market, a crisis may result. In the real world, each of our three Departments may represent a multiplicity of commodities and of firms, all of which will lead to further uncertainty as to whether the balancing conditions which keep the economy in an equilibrium of simple reproduction can always be met.

The two- and three-Departmental models as presented in Vol. II by Marx abstract from price considerations completely since everything is expressed in value terms. If, for example, Department II were to experience technological change, the quantity of labour required to produce wage goods may decline and therefore the value of a unit of labour power will decline. This will change the exchange ratio between Departments and will be reflected in the *amounts* of value exchanged in absolute terms.

Simple reproduction is not a realistic assumption since it is in the nature of a capitalist system not to stand still. Even when aggregate data (e.g., GNP) show zero growth, there will be changes in the value ratios due to continuous changes in tastes or technology. In any case, what we observe is a fluctuating growth rate and continuous net accumulation in observed data about capitalist countries. We recast our schema in terms of Expanded Reproduction. In each period, the surplus value is realized in money terms and reinvested in constant as well as variable capitals on an expanded scale. Thus, for example, in the context of System (1) above, C_1 next year will incorporate a part of S_1 of this year and will therefore exceed C_1 of this year. Such expansion of C_1 and V_1 as we see here is in value terms and may mean even a greater expansion of physical quantities since values are always changing, especially because the value of labour power is always sought to be reduced. The logic of the system which drives it to expand continuously is embodied in the behaviour of the rate of profit and the rate of exploitation. We shall discuss this next and postpone any discussion of Expanded Reproduction.

THE RATE OF EXPLOITATION AND THE RATE OF PROFIT

In terms of value relations which Marx treats as crucial to understanding the class division in capitalist society, surplus value and the rate of exploitation are the key variables. At the level of observed data, profits and the rate of profit on capital are the key variables. The desire for profits drives the capitalist to seek as large a difference between M and M' as possible. On certain assumptions (which have to be always kept in mind) one can talk of the rate of profit in value terms. These simplifying assumptions comprise the conditions under which prices are strictly proportional to values in each Department and in each firm within each industry. Much confusion has been caused by the ambiguities with regard to this concept and due to the fact that in Vol. I of *Capital*, Marx talks in terms of the (value) rate of profit. In the latter two volumes the money rate of profit is distinguished, but here again Marx made a number of simple but serious errors in solving the price-value transformation problem. We shall try as far as possible to confine the term rate of profit to the price domain but add the parenthetical word (value) when we talk about the simple case. A number of puzzles regarding Marx's predictions especially regarding 'the falling rate of profit' will be clarified (but not necessarily solved) by adhering strictly to this distinction.

The rate of exploitation is the ratio of surplus value to variable capital; it measures that part of the value generated by labour which is expropriated by the capitalist. The worker works for the full working day and creates more value than is embodied in the amount of variable capital advanced in securing his services. Various factors influence the rate of exploitation or the rate of surplus value. These are also influenced by circumstances such as the course of the class struggle - strikes, workers' solidarity, degree of unionisation, the nature of the ruling government, as well as technological innovations, availability of cheap sources of raw materials and foodstuffs either by trade or conquest etc. The capitalist acts to maximise the rate of surplus value which in turn influences the rate of profit. The influence can be shown directly in terms of the (value) rate of profit and is much more indirect in terms of the observable rate of profit. The direct influence is mediated by the organic composition of capital.

The organic composition of capital which is also a value concept is the proportion of constant capital in the sum of total capital advanced or $C_i/(C_i + V_i)$ where i refers to any particular individual firm/industry/Department. Only under certain (unlikely) circumstances can this be approximated by the ratio of physical quantities of men and machines assuming that these can be added together at all $(MP_i/L_i + MP_i)$ nor is this the money value of fixed capital as a ratio of the money value of fixed capital and the wage bill.[1] The ratio illustrates the importance of class relations since whereas the capitalist needs labour power in the productive process, he controls more easily the objective factor - materials of production. The buying and selling of MP involves transactions *within* the class which has a monopoly of means of production and hence such transactions do not involve antagonistic conflicts (though there may be cut-throat competition). In purchasing labour power, the capitalist confronts the worker not just as one individual to another entering in exchange but as members of two different and antagonistic *classes* one of which has a monopoly of means of production and the other has been divested of these means. The ratio has thus a qualitative, social dimension to it {82}.

Quantitatively, the organic composition of capital (g) is important because the (value) rate of profit can be related to the rate of surplus value (r) through g. Very simply, we define the (value) rate of profit (p) as the ratio of surplus value to the sum of capital advanced. $S_i/(C_i + V_i)$. In terms of only one good, we have

$$p = \frac{S}{C + V} = \frac{S}{V}\left(1 - \frac{C}{C + V}\right)$$

$$p = r(1 - g) \tag{3}$$

The simplicity of this formula is misleading and an invitation to indiscriminate application of it. For the present we notice that the rate of profit varies directly with the rate of surplus value (r) and inversely with the organic composition of capital (g). Thus the within-class transactions which determine g depress the rate of profit and the antagonistic class transaction helps it. To a Hegelian philosopher, this is a dialectical relationship rich with possibilities and Marx weaves fascinating patterns from it. We shall proceed however to relate these value concepts to the quantities which are observable - those which are in the domain of prices and exchange.

PRICES AND VALUES: THE TRANSFORMATION PROBLEM

An Historical Introduction

The problem of values and prices - the transformation problem - has been at the heart of the controversy regarding Marx's theory. For many critics of Marx, his failure to show that prices are proportional to values is a sufficient reason for abandoning his entire apparatus. Bohm-Bawerk in his *Karl Marx and the Close of his System*[1] was the first to point out that Marx had asserted that prices are proportional to values in Vol. I of *Capital* and promised to show this solution explicitly which he failed to do. In Vol. III, Marx was stuck with an example where prices in the different Departments were not proportional to values. Bohm-Bawerk in his brilliant polemical work was able to show that the various reasons Marx advanced in order to salvage this result were not adequate. Values if they were based on labour content alone could not according to him explain prices and profits in the real world. If labour values could not explain the structure of prices and profits, then the theory of surplus value which asserted that capitalism was based on the exploitation of workers also fell. Clearly it was Marx's failure to take into account the contribution of the other factors of production which seemed to be at the heart of this failure.

A few years before Bohm-Bawerk's criticism (which had to wait until all the three volumes of *Capital* were published), Philip Wick-steed[2] in a celebrated debate with Bernard Shaw had demonstrated that relative prices were in fact explained by relative scarcities and therefore by the ratio of marginal utilities which they yielded to a

consumer. Wicksteed's demonstration did not deal in detail with Marx's
theory but showed that an explanation based on Jevons' theory of utility was a superior logical explanation. If prices are explained by
relative scarcity rather than by labour content, then the notion of
surplus value ceases to have rational foundation. Profits become a
legitimate income as a reward for relative scarcity of capital.
(Bernard Shaw was to admit the force of this argument and later in his
life concentrated on the Ricardian notion of land rent as unearned
surplus. To this day land nationalisation and appropriation of profits
in real estate have been a part of the Labour Party's economic philo-
sophy. Profits in industrial activities are regarded as legitimate).

The importance of Wicksteed's criticism has been underrated. In
Neoclassical economics, the duality of exchange value and use value
is accepted. But whereas in Classical and Marxian theory these two
are independent of each other, in Neoclassical economic theory, they
are linked together causally. This was the crucial new element in
Jevons' contribution that Wicksteed uses to criticise Marx. Marx's
explanation of exploitation relies on the independent determination
of the exchange value of labour power and the use value of labour
during the production process. The marginalist and the modern approach
denies this independence and causally links the two via the twin
prongs of disutility of work and the productivity of labour. It
treats labour and capital as symmetrical with all commodities and
thus does not employ the notion of class relations in the labour
market any more than in the commodity market.

The Marxist reply to these criticisms has not been very convinc-
ing. Many like Hyndman have been polemical and have relied on
assertions without proof.[3] They argued that Marx was speaking of
values as long run or natural prices; considerations of demand/supply
which modern economics takes into account are only relevant to short
run prices. This does not at all meet Bohm-Bawerk's point which did
relate to such long run prices. Many repeated the arguments advanced
by Marx which Bohm-Bawerk had already dealt with. There grew a gulf
between Marx's theory and modern economic theory with very little
communication between them.

As we shall show later, Marx's attempt to solve the transformation problem was marred by some simple but very serious errors. It was up to Bortkiewicz to correctly formulate the problem Marx was attempting to solve and show the nature of the solution. Bortkiewicz correctly saw that the problem had to be formulated separately in price terms and in value terms and then a 'mapping' from values to prices had to be rigorously established.

Bortkiewicz's solution[4] was mathematically elegant but he did not use any of the tools that modern developments in linear algebra have made available to economics. His solution was published in German in 1906-1907 but did not become available in English until 1948. By then, von Neumann's growth model was also available in English and was the most general formulation of the linear economic model.[5] The linear model has a number of parallels with Marx's formulations and hence the mathematical properties of the linear model can be directly used to analyse Marx's model.

During the 1930's, there was a revival of interest in Marxian economics but this was more on the macroeconomic contributions of Marx. This was because Keynes' General Theory had provided economists with a 'new pair of glasses' for reading Marx. There was much interesting writing on Marxian theory of cycles and of Marx's pioneering contribution to national income analysis. The value problem was ignored in all these discussions.

In the late 1940's, Winternitz proposed a solution of the value price transformation problem using the notion of linear models.[6] Samuelson in his 1957 article explicitly treated the value scheme as an input-output model and confirmed many of the criticisms of Bohm-Bawerk and the analysis of Bortkiewicz.[7] This was that values and prices could be proportional only if either (i) equal rates of exploitation among industries and equal organic composition of capital prevailed, or (ii) zero rate of exploitation and zero rate of profit prevailed everywhere. We shall demonstrate this later.

There has been an upsurge of interest in Marx again in the 1970's. Samuelson has returned to the question of transformation problem in his 1971 article in the Journal of Economic Literature.[8] This article, which we shall discuss in greater detail later, argues that the value price transformation is an unnecessary step, that the value scheme is applicable only to very simple economies and is an erroneous view of the economic system. Morishima, on the other hand, has arrived at somewhat different conclusions using the same tools.[9] Starting with a clear distinction between the value and the price models, he has tried to formulate Marx's propositions in mathematically rigorous fashion. His analysis, which we shall examine later, concludes with the message that the labour theory of value can be superseded today by better mathematical formulations.

Since our interpretation of the labour theory of value differs considerably from that of these writings, we shall first outline the problem as treated by Marx and Bortkiewicz. We shall then examine Marx's errors and Bortkiewicz's solution in the light of our interpretation. We will then survey the contributions of other writers to bring out the differences more sharply.

VALUES AND PRICES: THE PROBLEM AS POSED BY MARX[1]

The simplest way to pose the transformation problem is as follows.
Marx states that surplus value can be generated only by living labour
i.e. by the exploitation of the labourer by the capitalist. If that
is true, surplus value and hence profit should be higher in those
industries where the ratio of labour power to materials of production
is high and vice versa. But everyone, including Marx, accepts that the
rate of profit is constant across industries. Here is a basic contradiction.

Marx's formulation of the problem is in terms of five industries
(or capitals as he calls them) but can be cast in terms of equation (2)
above. He assumed in every solution that he offered that the rate of
exploitation (r) was the same in every industry. He also accepted that
the rate of profit as a mark up above the sum of constant and variable
capital was also the same for every industry. But given identical
rates of surplus value, profit rates could be identical in all industries only if the organic composition of capital was the same. This
is shown trivially by our equation (3) above.

In his solution in Vol. III, Marx made two further assumptions.
He first assumed that the total *amount* of profits (R) was equal to the
total *amount* of surplus value (S) generated. Secondly, he assumed
that the average rate of profit in each industry (or Department) was
equal to the ratio of total surplus value to the total value of constant capital and variable capital. In terms of equations (1) or (2),
this says that the average rate of profit $\bar{p}$ (we call it $\bar{p}$ since it is
ambiguous yet whether this is a value rate or a price rate) equals
$S/(C + V)$. In effect the second assumption is a consequence of the first.

45

Making these two assumptions, Marx arrived at the result that prices deviated from values. He seems to advance explanations for this result by saying that the drive towards making the rate of profit in every industry equal to the average rate of profit made some prices more than proportionate to values while others were less so. If the organic composition of capital in an industry was above the 'average' aggregate ratio, then price was above value and vice versa. The industry whose organic composition reflected the average aggregate ratio had price proportional to value. This however made obvious the *direct* relation between prices (and hence profits) and the organic composition of capital and hence the contribution of other, i.e. non-labour, inputs in explaining profits. Let us study Marx's solution at this stage. We formulate this in terms of the three Department scheme in (2) above.

TABLE I

Formal Representation of Marx's Price-Value Scheme

Dept.	Constant Capital	Variable Capital	Surplus Value	Total Value Produced	Rate of Surplus Value	Average Rate of Profit	Total Output in Price Terms
I	C_1	V_1	S_1	Y_1	$S_1 = r_1 V_1$	$S/C + V$	$(1+\bar{p})(C_1 + V_1) =$
II	C_2	V_2	S_2	Y_2	$S_2 \ r_2 V_2$	$S/C + V$	$(1+\bar{p})(C_2 + V_2) =$
III	C_3	V_3	S_3	Y_3	$S_3 \ r_3 V_3$	$S/C + V$	$(1+\bar{p})(C_3 + V_3) =$
	C	V	S	Y			

(Note that each Department's equation can be interpreted also in per unit of output' terms).

For each Department.

$$Y_i = C_i + (1 + r_i) \ V_i \tag{4}$$

$$P_i = (1 + \bar{p})(C_i + V_i) \tag{5}$$

Marx's assumptions connecting value and prices are (i) $r_i = r$,
(ii) $S = (S_1 + S_2 + S_3) = rV = \bar{p}\Sigma(C_i + V_i) = R =$ Total Profits. (6)
Since by definition (a) $C_i/(C_i + V_i) = g_i$, (b) $C/(C +V) = g$ and
(c) $\bar{p} = S/(C + V).$, we have

$$Y_i = \left[\frac{g_i + (1 - g_i)(1 + r)}{(1 - g_i)} \right] V_i \tag{7}$$

$$P_i = \frac{(1 + \bar{p})}{(1 - g_i)} V_i \tag{8}$$

$$P_i/Y_i = \frac{1 + r(1 - g)}{1 + r(1 - g_i)} \tag{9}$$

Now for prices to be proportional to values in every Department, the
ratio P_i/Y_i must be equal across Departments. This can be true *either*
if $r = 0$ and $\bar{p} = 0$, i.e. no exploitation and no profits, *or* if all
the g_i are equal to g i.e. only if the organic composition of capital
is the same in every Department. When these conditions are not met,
we can see from (4) that if $g_i > g$, $P_i/Y_i > 1$ and vice versa. Thus
prices deviate from values by this equation if the organic compositions
of capital differ.

This result is thought to be very damaging for the labour theory
of value.[2] The impossibility of deriving prices which are proportional
to values has led some to urge the abandonment of the labour theory of
value. They feel that the important parts of Marx's contributions
are over-shadowed by this error. A redressing of Marx in modern
clothes - in terms of modern economic theory - has been attempted by
many economists. Before we evaluate these attempts, let us understand
the nature of Marx's error.

Marx's fundamental error was to treat value relations as if they
are observable and directly measurable. The gap between value relations and price relations is what causes value relations to be not
directly observable in the commodity mode of production. By writing
down the scheme as in equation (2) or in Table I, value categories are
treated as if the individual capitalist and the individual worker could
directly perceive the relations of exploitation. The scheme in

47

Table I is also a commodity-commodity (C' - C') circuit and neglects the monetary aspects. The importance of M - M' circuit lies in the fact that since the capitalist has to sell his output, he has to realize surplus value - convert it into money. It is only at this level of exchange that relationships can be observed. What the capitalist sees however is not the *value* of constant capital or variable capital; he sees material *costs* and a wage bill. These values and costs are identical only if all the prices are proportional to values. The capitalist cannot add $\bar p$ to his value sum of capital. He wants to make a rate of profit (in price terms) - call it ρ to distinguish it from p and $\bar p$ such that $M' = (1 + \rho)M$. Thus Marx has forgotten his discussion in Vol. I and in Chapter I of Vol. III about the nature of commodity fetishism. In order to pose the problem correctly and derive conclusions regarding the nature of social relations we must reformulate the price-value problem, strictly adhering to the rule that value relations are unobservable. We immediately move to the solution proposed by Ladislaus von Bortkiewicz who reformulated and correctly solved the problem in Table I.

VALUES AND PRICES: THE PROBLEM AS SOLVED BY BORTKIEWICZ[1]

Bortkiewicz correctly recognised that the cost-price equation for P_i must have both sides in price terms. Thus the value of constant capital must be multiplied by the price of constant capital and similarly for variable capital and surplus value. He chose a different rule for linking up the value equations and price equations. As we shall see later, this rule is crucial to the social interpretation of the transformation problem.

Let the price of Department I be p_1, of II be p_2 and of III be p_3. Let us call the rate of profit (now appropriately a concept defined in the price domain) ρ. All Departments make this rate. Then corresponding to the value equations of Table I we have

$$p_1 C = (1 + \rho)(p_1 C_1 + p_2 V_1) \tag{10a}$$

$$p_2 V = (1 + \rho)(p_1 C_2 + p_2 V_2) \tag{10b}$$

$$p_3 S = (1 + \rho)(p_1 C_3 + p_2 V_3) \tag{10c}$$

$(p_1 C_1 + p_2 V_1)$ is now the cost of production on money terms $(\dot{M})$ for Department I; when the output is sold, the capitalist hopes to convert C' into M' where competition ensures that M' = $(1 + \rho)$M. The value equations are as before

$$Y_i = C_i + (1 + r)V_i$$

or $$Y_i = \frac{g_i + (1 - g_i)(1 + r)}{(1 - g_i)} V_i$$

49

where $g_i = C_i/(C_i + V_i)$ and r is the rate of exploitation assumed to be equal across industries.

Instead of the condition that total surplus value is equal to total profits in the economy, Bortkiewicz introduces a rule that prices are so chosen that the total value of output (Y) equals the total output in price terms

$$p_1 C + p_2 V + p_3 S = C + V + S = Y = Y_1 + Y_2 + Y_3 \qquad (11)$$

Given equations (10a)-(10c) and (11), we have four unknowns, p_1, p_2, p_3, and ρ. Notice again that the price of Department III's output does not enter into cost calculations of any of the three Departments. Department III represents luxury goods or gold and we start by re-defining all prices relative to the price of Department III. We set $p_3 = 1$. Given now three unknowns, these can be solve in terms of g_i, r, and V_i. We get the following answers

$$p_1 = \frac{p_2(1-g_1)(1+\rho)}{g_1 + (1+r)(1-g_1) - (1+\rho)g_1} \qquad (12)$$

$$p_2 = \frac{g_2 g_3 + g_2(1+r)(1-g_3)}{g_2 g_3 + (1+r)(1-g_2) + (g_2 - g_3)(1+\rho)} \qquad (13)$$

$$(1+\rho) = \frac{[1+(1+r)(1-g_1)] - \{[1+(1+r)(1-g_1)]\}^2}{2(g_1 - g_2)}$$

$$+ \frac{rg_2[(1-g_1)(1+r)g_1-(1-g_1)rg_1 g_2+(1+r)^2(1-g_1)]^2\}^{\frac{1}{2}}}{2(g_1 - g_2)} \qquad (14)$$

These answers look complicated but we reproduce numerical examples in Table II which will contrast the Marx and Bortkiewicz answers. Before we look at the answers in numerical terms let us look at the meaning of equations (12)-(14). To begin with we see that the rate of profit is defined in terms r, g_1 and g_2. Since we have taken p_3 to be the numeraire, no price term appears explicitly in the rate of profit equation. It is necessary that $g_1 > g_2$ i.e. the organic composition of capital in Department I should be greater than that in Department II. Once the rate of profit is defined then p_2 is defined in terms

g_2, g_3, r and ρ whereas p_1 is defined in terms of p_2, g_1, r and ρ. Notice that g_3 the organic composition of capital in Department III does not affect the rate of profit.

Table II gives Bortkiewicz's original numerical examples and shows how Marx forumlated the problem in value terms and derived his erroneous price solutions. *Bortkiewicz's solution illustrates how the dissolution of surplus value into profit is accomplished by the price mechanism.* It is hard to measure, say, the organic composition of capital from the price data. Looking at price data which are readily observable, one might measure g_1 as 288/(288 + 96) or 3/4. but this would be erroneous because the true value of g_1 is 5/7. Similarly the ratio of profit $(p_3 s_i)$ to wage bill $(p_2 v_i)$ in any sector does not measure 'true' rate of exploitation. Starting from equal rates of exploitation in value terms, we observe different ratios of profits to wages in price terms. Thus Bortkiewicz clearly shows that Marx's value categories cannot be measured directly from observed price data. It is not legitimate therefore to think of the organic composition of capital in terms of capital-labour ratio of modern economic theory. We shall keep this dimension of the price-value problem in mind when we come to discussing the question of testing Marx's predictions, e.g. the falling rate of profit.

TABLE II

Numerical Examples of Value-Price Problem

	Value Relations				Marx's Price Equations	Bortkiewicz's Price Equations			
	c_i	v_i	s_i	Y_i	P_i	$p_1 c_i$	$p_2 v_i$	$p_3 s_i$	
I	225	90	60	375	(1+8/27)(225+9)) =408.333	288	96	96	480
II	100	120	80	300	(1+8/27)(100+120)=285.185	128	128	64	320
III	50	90	60	200	(1+8/27)(50+90) =181.481	64	96	40	200
	375	300	200	875	875	480	320	200	1000

$g_1 = 225/315 = 0.714$ $P_1/Y_1 = 1.089$ $p_1 = 32/25 = 1.28$

$g_2 = 100/220 = 0.454$ $P_2/Y_2 = 0.951$ $p_2 = 16/15 = 1.07$

$g_3 = 50/140 = 0.357$ $P_3/Y_3 = 0.907$ $\rho = 1/4 = 0.25$

$g = 300/675 = 0.555$ $r = 2/3$ $\bar{p} = \dfrac{200}{675} = \dfrac{8}{27}$

51

We recall that whereas Marx had a condition that total profits equal total surplus value, Bortkiewicz's condition was different. By setting p_3 = 1, Bortkiewicz implicitly imposes the same condition but a different normalization rule would produce different magnitudes. When we come to a discussion of expanded reproduction, this difference will become clearer but its social implications need to be pointed out at this stage. Marx's condition implies that all profits arise from surplus value but also that surplus value goes only to profit receivers. In Bortkeiwicz's solution, the division of total value can be to profits or to wage bill as long as the total value identity is preserved. This is a very important consideration in studying the dynamics of modern capitalism. Let us discuss this a bit further.

The normalisation that p_3 = 1, means that profits in money terms are the output of Department III and since all surplus value is spent on that Department we have defined profits equal to surplus value tautologically. For Marx it was a basic social relationship - class monopoly of means of production - which gave all profits the character of surplus value. In general, however, Marx gave immense importance to class struggle in determining such things as the rate of exploitation and the organic composition of capital. One must not therefore regard r and g_i as technologically determinate constants, but as variables in which technology as much as social forces such as the course of the class struggle will figure as determining variables. A high rate of employment, a high degree of unionisation, international rivalry among national capitalists - all these could lead to a different division of total value between profits and wages. Bortkiewicz's formula allows for this to occur since the precise division of total product in the price domain can take a more flexible form. To be able to determine what the division would be, we would have to add the determining equations for r and g_i - making them functions of the social forces and technological constraints; only such an interpretation can help in understanding the course of modern capitalism.

Let us pursue a bit further the difference made by the normalization rule by Bortkiewicz in comparison to Marx. This difference is somewhat obscured by Bortkiewicz's choice of the numéraire. If for example, we choose as our deflator not p_3 but a general index (such as the GNP deflator), then the identity of surplus value and total profits breaks down in the Bortkiewicz formula. Usually, when 'testing' the validity of Marx's predictions, national income accounts in some 'constant price' terms are used. Such a deflator involves a normalization rule that p_1, p_2 and p_3 be weighted by some base year quantities and in terms of that deflator the Bortkiewicz identity [eqn. (11)] would hold. This deflator however will not then fulfill Marx's requirement that total profits equal total surplus value. Whereas usually the choice of a deflator or a normalization rule is a mathematically trivial operation, in this case. it makes a qualitative difference to the final computations and makes any testing of Marx's predictions from available data more difficult.[2]

VALUES AND PRICES.   WHY SOLVE THE PROBLEM AT ALL?

To many people, the transformation problem is a pedantic exercise indulged in by academic economists or by diehard Marxists each to prove his point but with no practical relevance. Under *some* set of assumptions, they say, it is doubtless easy to show that values are proportional to prices while under a variety of other assumptions, it would not be so. Our discussion in the previous section has shown one such set of assumptions ($g_i = g$, $r_i = r$) which will *solve* the problem.[1] The Bortkiewicz solution and Marx's own erroneous formulation in Vol. III of *Capital* are examples where prices are not proportional to values. Why does this matter?

The Bortkiewicz solution as contained in equations (12) to (14) above clearly shows that from value ratios such as g_i and r, one can solve for prices and the rate of profit. But he also shows clearly that prices are not proportional to values except under special conditions. Strict proportionality is a stronger requirement in this case; what is sufficient is that from g_i and r, prices should be determinable. As in the case of proofs of existence of General Equilibrium, to prove the existence of a price set given a set of value ratios should be adequate. Uniqueness of prices and, even more, strict proportionality of prices and values are much more stringent requirements. Prices in general are not proportional to values but can be derived from the latter. As a *technical* problem in economic theory, the transformation problem is thus disposed of by Bortkiewicz.

The social problem, however, remains and that indicates that the technical problem solved may not be the correct one. Prices are directly observable and one does not need any value information to know what they are. The categories of total costs - wage bill, material costs - and profits are also directly measurable. We need value theory to make sense of *why* prices and profits are what they are and thereby to understand why capitalist societies are ridden by inequality and class divisions. Since the commodity mode of production dissolves the social relation of value - surplus value and exploitation - and makes only prices and exchange visible, it is the task of a theorist to show that *one can go back to value relations given only price information*. The transformation problem can be posed in modern terms with which econometrics has. made us familiar. In terms of econometric theory, the price relations are observed *reduced form* equations whereas the value relations are the unobservable *structural form equations*. A test of the validity of a model (its identifiability) is that one should be able to go back from the reduced form to the structural form uniquely and vice versa. In Neoclassical economic theory, preferences and technology are the structural relations which explain the observed price-quantity data. Marx would reject these Neoclassical relations as not penetrating beneath the surface of exchange relationships to the relations of production and the forces of production. But Marx went further than this. He also emphasised that the observed reality was the inverse or mirror image of the true social relationship {21}{39}. Thus, exchange shows equality where the true relationships are of exploitation. In this sense, observed reality is upside down, and empirical data *unless approached within a value theoretic framework* would lead to conclusions which will contradict the predictions of the value theory. A solution of the transformation problem is important, therefore, for any quantitative empirical study seeking to understand the world in Marxian terms {21}.

The appropriate way the problem should be posed is to say that given price data (including costs, profits, etc.), can one solve for g_i and r? The reason for assuming equal rates of exploitation becomes transparent at this point. It is not a 'behavioural' rule, *nor is it a necessary part of Marx's value theory*.[3] It is a way of reducing the number of unknowns in the transformation problem from six (three g_i and three r_i.) to four, since the four equations in the price domain can only solve for four unknowns. If the rates of exploitation differed from one industry to another and the organic composition did as well but the rate of profit was equal across industries, then the explanation of 'dissolving' of value relations becomes very complex. Why is this so?

The role of price mechanism and exchange in Marx's theory is to mask surplus value and make it appear legitimate as profit. The profit of any one particular firm, industry or Department does not equal the surplus value produced by it. The equalisation of the rate of profit across industries in price terms means that price movements and 'behavioural' decisions of capitalists regarding choice of techniques etc. can be seen as equalising profit rates. But equal rates of profit and the implied relative price movements mean that profits of one industry may comprise of surplus values of many other industries from whom it buys and to whom it sells. The link between profits and surplus value becomes complex and in fighting against exploitation workers cannot fight against their own industry's owners in isolation; they have to fight the whole system. The price mechanism thus divides up total surplus value into profits of different industries such that rates of profit are equal. (There is a further division of profits into interest, ground rent, etc., which Marx discusses in Vol. III). The condition that total surplus value equals total profits is not just another equation but a way in which, for Marx, the price and value systems are linked up.

For Bortkiewicz, the price mechanism has the role of allocating total value produced into different incomes (wages, profits, etc.) and different total revenue after sale for each Department in such a way that the rate of profit is equal. The link between surplus value and profits is made even more indirect. In the particular example chosen above, as we have said before, the arbitrary rule is that $p_3 = 1$. This plus the stipulation that all surplus value is spent as revenue on the output of Department III brings out the same identity of total value and total profits as in Marx. But if the capitalists were to spend a part of their surplus value on wage goods produced by Department II or partly accumulate, this identity would no longer hold. Surplus value cannot be identified *even in the aggregate* by looking at total profits. At each stage, the transformation problem has to be solved anew to decompose profits, wages and other costs into constant capital, variable capital and surplus value. Unless this is done in an analytical fashion, any talk of high profits being a sign of exploitation remains unscientific. To say that workers are exploited because profits are high may have moral force for some but it is not a scientific statement as Marx would insist it should be. Bortkiewicz's condition, while making the problem more complex, is more general since the inter-dependence of values and prices becomes total though not inseparable. A Marxian analysis cannot rely on data on wages and profits or on a 'capital-labour' ratio to prove exploitation; and as a corollary, the absence of exploitation is also not proven by any data on constancy of wage shares or of rising real wages or the ratio of wages to average product. All these are data from the price domain and do not shed light on categories from the value domain unless the transformation is carried out to value relations.

XII

ALTERNATIVE APPROACHES TO THE PROBLEM

Our interpretation of the role of value theory in Marx emphasises the unobservable nature of the value relationship. Commodity fetishism is the process that disguises the social relationships of value and brings to the fore exchange relationships between commodities. In his discussions on the exchange of money for labour power and of the wage form Marx explicitly brings out this masking of social or value relationships. The modern approach to Marx in the writings of Samuelson, Morishima and others is quite different from our approach. Fetishism and class struggle are much underplayed, if not ignored, as part of Marx's sociology separable from the economic theoretic model of values and prices. The transition from values to prices is mediated in this approach by the input-output table. Such a table provides information on commodity inputs and labour inputs used in producing each commodity output. The materials of production (in Marx's terminology) are broken down into the many constituent commodities and the labour input is measured in terms of labour time. Marx's own discussion of the commodity circuit of capital lends some support to this interpretation {71}. This approach then uses the input-output table to describe the technology of production - the 'physical' conditions of production. It is then shown by these authors in only slightly different ways that prices can be derived from an input-output table assuming equal rates of profit in each industry. But from this analysis, different authors have come to different conclusions.

There are several parallels between the mathematical structure of Marx's value equations as written in the analysis of simple reproduction (Table I above) and the Leontieff input-output system. Indeed, the

Leontieff system may have derived from the strong Russian tradition
in Marxian economics which saw attempts by many economists and
mathematicians such as Dimitriev, Bortkiewicz, Tugan-Baranowsky and
others to pose Marx's value and accumulation problem mathematically.[1]
The input-output interpretation of Marx's value theory has the simultaneous advantage of translating Marx in modern economic terms and
using all the available results concerning the mathematical structure
of linear models. These results can treat generally both simple and
expanded reproduction.

The assumption necessary to make the value - input translation is
that of constant technology in the sense of given constant output coefficients. We also need a notion of constant productivity of labour
so that a unit of value of labour power can be translated in terms of
a unit of labour time. We also need to assume, as in the C' - C'
circuit, that the requisite amounts of inputs are always readily
available to convert output back into material inputs and labour power.
Similarly, when translating physical input-output relations into price
relations we have to assume that there is no problem of realizing
total value and especially surplus value. The problem of selling
output - converting commodity - capital C' into money M' is subsumed
away in this scheme. Whereas Marx ignored these only in setting up
his table for simple reproduction but always reminded his readers of
these complications time and again, these authors concentrate on
Marx's tables which incorporate these assumptions but underplay the
other complications, especially regarding the role of money as money
capital in the capitalist system.

Authors who have discussed Marx's value theory frequently disagree in their assessment of his importance as an economist. They have
tried to evaluate him within the terms of the Economics paradigm, i.e.
in terms of the concerns of mainstream economic theory and its approach.
Most authors however are agreed that whereas Marx may have pioneered
the formulations of certain problems, the apparatus of labour theory of
value which he used is inadequate, cumbersome and logically faulty.
Morishima, for example, in his recent work tackles Marx's system very
sympathetically and proves a number of Marxian propositions with the
help of advanced mathematical techniques. He ultimately finds however

that the only way to incorporate Marx's insights into modern economics is to discard the labour theory of value in favour of a more general model in terms of physical input-output relations and price-wage-profit relations. The concerns of these many attempts are more with the problems in modern economic theory and in integrating Marx back into the tradition. Their discussion is also mathematically advanced. We remark here on these theories in the light of our previous discussions.

The mathematical translation of values into physical input-output coefficients enables Morishima in particular to pose the output-price duality explicitly. Morishima derives an expression for the rate of exploitation (assumed as constant) in terms of the labour time contained in the basket of wage earners.

While Winternitz and May in their respective notes had discussed Bortkiewicz's solution and its generality, it was Samuelson who in his article on Marx in 1957 explicitly set out the Marxian scheme as an input-output table. He directly identified variable capital with wage bill and expressed it as the money wage rate (w) times labour input. Similarly, he directly identified the constant capital as the price of a unit of capital - the output of Department I times the physical quantity of capital. In thus setting out Marx's scheme, Samuelson implicitly defined Marx's value categories as price categories. His categories of wage bill, intermediate inputs and costs - all in money terms - are then separated into price and quantity. Samuelson was then able to derive his prices from physical input-output coefficients directly without posing the value problem at all. "Yet, the present *exact* analysis suggests that this so-called 'transformation problem' is rather pointless." The value scheme is, indeed, entirely irrelevant to the problem Samuelson solves. Let us study it in some detail.

In order to distinguish Marx's value units and Samuelson's physical quantities, we shall retain Samuelson's notation as far as possible. The physical output of Department I is labelled K (corresponding to Marxian value concept C) and the physical output of Department II is labelled Y (corresponding to Marxian value concept V but not to be confused with the Y_1, Y_2 or Y above in Table I). The price of K is p_1 and the price of Y is p_2. The total output of Department I in terms of money flows is then p_1K and of Department II p_2Y. The analogy here with Bortkiewicz's equations (10a)-(10c) is obvious though Bortkiewicz did not employ the notion of physical quantities. Now an input-output scheme can be made for the two Departments as follows:

Department	I	II	Final Demand	Total Gross Output
I	$p_1 K_1$	$p_1 K_2$	0	$(p_1 K) = \Sigma$
II	0	0	$p_2 Y$	$(p_2 Y) = \Sigma^*$
Wages	wL_1	wL_2		
Interest	$\rho(wL_1 + p_1 K_1)$	$\rho(wL_2 + p_1 K_2)$		
Total costs	Σ	Σ^*	Σ^*	

The table can be read across each row or each column. Thus the first row shows that the output of Department I goes partly to Department I $(p_1 K_1)$ or to Department II $(p_1 K_2)$. There is no sale of K to any consumers hence final demand for Department I is zero. Reading down column II, we see that in producing Y, $p_1 K_2$ is used as an input but no inputs from Department II are used. Output of Department II consisting of wage goods is sold entirely to consumers as final demand. Reading further down Column II we see that the other inputs (or costs since they are in money terms) are labour appearing as wage costs and what Samuelson calls 'interest' or could be called profits which is the rate of profit ρ times the input costs $p_1 K_2 + wL_2$. The columns incorporating costs and a rate of profit are also analogous to Bortkiewitcz's equations. The difference is in treatment V as an input in Marx and as final demand here; on the other hand, labour input L is introduced explicitly with a wage rate attached to it.

If one were to divide each element in each row by total output, we get the input requirement for each Department's output in each column. Thus in the Samuelson scheme we have (K_1/K) as the requirement of machine goods input per unit of output of machine goods. But, rather than derive the input-output matrix in such terms, Samuelson describes the technology in physical terms as follows:

$$a_1 K + a_2 Y = L$$
$$b_1 K + b_2 Y = K$$

it takes a_2 units of labour and b_2 units of capital to produce one unit of Y and a_1 units of labour and b_1 units of capital to produce one unit of K. The equations above describe how the total supply of each input is assigned to either producing K or Y.

This technology together with the total cost equations solves the two ratios p_1/w, p_2/w given p. Thus, analogous to the price value equations of Bortkiewicz (12)-(14) above, we get

$$\frac{p_1}{w} = \frac{a_1(1 + p)}{1 - b_1(1 + p)}$$

$$\frac{p_2}{w} = \frac{a_2(1 + p)[1 - b_1(1 + p)] + a_1(1 + p)b_2(1 + p)}{1 - b_1(1 + p)}$$

Notice that in this scheme w and p are given from outside the system. Since w/p_2 is the real wage ratio, one can say that given the profit rate p, the real wage rate and the price of machine goods are determined by technology.

Samuelson is thus solving the problem of deriving relative prices from technological coefficients. His interpretation of Marxian value theory is therefore as a theory of relative prices. Given unchanging technology in the form of a_1, a_2, b_1, b_2 coefficients; given a money wage rate w and a profit rate p, the prices p_1 and p_2 can be solved. Since he has no identity for total value and total price or surplus profits, the profit rate is determined outside Samuelson's system of equations.

The value equations are irrelevant here because the class relations are ignored. The length of working day or the level of real wage is determined not by strikes or unions but by technology. Samuelson's interpretation of Marx is thus technologically deterministic. We have already cited Marx several times above to indicate the importance of changing value relations, changing technology and of the class struggle as well as of technology to make clear that Samuelson's analysis must be regarded as a very narrow view of Marx.

In his later article in the *Journal of Economic Literature* Samuelson returned to this problem. He once again tackled the labour theory of value as a theory of relative prices and his analysis confirmed his earlier conclusions.

These are:

(a) In simple economies where production does not use any produced means of production but only labour, prices are proportional to labour content. This is the example that Adam Smith uses regarding "early and rude state" where only deer and beaver are produced.

(b) If labour and materials of production are both required, we have an input-output system where direct as well as indirect labour input has to be taken into account. In this case the labour contained in the produced means of production must be weighted by the ruling rate of profit. Thus if as in Samuelson's example the economy produces beaver coats from beaver skin obtained earlier and then some time is spent sewing the beaver skin. The price of a beaver coat would then depend on the direct labour input of sewing the beaver skin and the indirect labour input of killing the beaver. In other words, the labour content of means of production is the indirect labour content. For prices to cover the ruling rate of profit, this indirect labour content must be compounded by the rate of profit. This analysis is still in terms of physical input coefficients and derives prices from this information.

Samuelson thus poses the problem of prices in fairly simple terms to demonstrate Bortkiewicz's point that a profit rate must be used in calculating prices and that only under very special assumptions are prices proportional to labour content. This is a criticism of the classical labour theory of value. As such, no notion of exploitation is needed to calculate prices. In order to incorporate the rate of exploitation, Samuelson assumes, not a class division as Marx does, but a Malthusian population growth which drives wages to subsistence level. Population grows when wages rise above subsistence. The rate of exploitation in such a society is equal to the ratio of the difference between labour's product and the real wage rate and the real wage rate itself.

But this is not a Marxian model and, as Samuelson himself says, this calculus can only be true for a slave society. Marx rejected the Malthusian population theory because he was seeking an explanation for the level of real wages in the social rather than biological forces. Wicksteed saw this point quite clearly in his original review of *Capital*

referred to above. In this slave society, Samuelson's model shows
that the rate of profit ρ lies between zero and the rate of exploitation (defined according to Samuelson's model) and the forces of population growth are crucial in determining where they lie. Capitalists
(or slave owners) accumulate just enough to equip labour (slaves) with
the same amount of capital per capita. Since there is no assumption
of continuous technical change, there is no drive on the part of
capitalists to accumulate continuously. The technology is static and
Malthus assures a steady supply of labour. In this world, real wages
rise only when the capitalists accumulate faster than the required
rate or if there is any technical change. There is no role for the
labourers to struggle for higher wages: they must rely either upon
the thriftiness of the capitalists or an exogenous technical change
falling like manna from heaven.

Samuelson also shows in addition that the value scheme proposed
by Marx can also be made consistent with the physical technology
matrix. Thus we have output-value transformation and output price
transformation which can be independent of each other. Once again a
subsistence wage rate has to be assumed as well as given technical
coefficients. Now a given subsistence real wage rate and a constant
productivity of labour allow Samuelson to transform value sums into
units of labour time and then into physical quantities. Prices are
totally irrelevant here because no exchange is involved at any stage.
We are still in the commodity circuit of capital. The Marxian value
theory in this context is indistinguishable from the classical labour
theory of value.

Of the two transformations - output-price and output-value - one
can choose one and discard the other according to Samuelson. In a
world of subsistence wage and constant technology, it is not surprising
that you do not need to know about value relations in order to derive
prices. Since the task of labour theory of value for Samuelson is to
solve for relative prices and quantities, value relations in the sense
of Marx are irrelevant. Samuelson also leaves out many aspects of
Marxian dynamics - realization problems, the role of money capital,
the influence of accumulation on real wages and the reserve army of
labour and of changing value relations. He does however clarify that

64

as a theory of prices or as a theory of resource allocation, the labour theory of value is redundant. In our view, it would be mistaken for Marxists to insist that Marx's theory can do the multiple tasks of providing a theory of prices, a theory of resource allocation and a theory of social relations in a capitalist economy. (In this context we do not discuss here the attempts by Soviet and Eastern European economists to use the labour theory of value as a planning tool. We will only mention that the view taken here is that Marx's theory is a tool for a critical study of capitalism, not an operational tool for socialist planning).

In his recent book, Morishima has treated the value-price problem in great detail. Morishima attempts to show that modern mathematical tools can be used to formulate Marx's theories rigorously and that such an attempt would confirm Marx's status as an outstanding economist of great originality.

Morishima's book has the merit of treating Marx sympathetically. He recognises that Marx's concern was to study how values became transformed into prices in capitalism rather than to establish any strict proportionality. Commenting on Samuelson's 1957 article, Morishima says "However, in the transformation problem Marx did not intend to establish a proportionality between values and prices but, on the contrary, to show that individual exploitation and individual profit are disproportional unless some restrictive conditions are imposed" (p.85).

Morishima begins by distinguishing two definitions of value in capital. One is the total amount of labour time crystallised in a commodity which is equal to the amount of labour crystallised in the commodities making up the means of production and the amount of direct labour input. Thus if λ_1 is the value of corn in terms of labour time and it takes corn, compost and labour in certain proportions to produce corn, we have

$$\lambda_1 = a_{11}\lambda_1 + a_{21}\lambda_2 + L_1$$

where $a_{11}\lambda_1$ is the labour time embodied in the corn output, $a_{21}\lambda_2$ the labour time embodied in the compost input and L_1 the direct labour

input. Alternatively, one could define value in terms of socially
necessary labour time. Thus the socially necessary labour time for
producing one unit of net output of corn is equal to the amount of
time necessary for producing the gross corn output and the compost
which go in as inputs.

$$\mu_1 = L_1 q_1 + L_2 q_2$$

$L_1 q_1$ being hours of labour employed in the corn industry and $L_2 q_2$ in
the compost industry required to produce μ_1 value of corn in labour
time. There is thus a duality according to Morishima between the
value determination system (λ) and the input-output calculus of
socially necessary labour (μ). Morishima then sets out the general
problem of duality in terms of many commodities.

In order to keep our discussion brief and mathematically as simple
as possible, we shall not go into all the details of the book but
concentrate on Morishima's treatment of the transformation problem.
Like Samuelson, Morishima recognises the trinity of value system,
physical input-output system and price system. Unlike Samuelson, he
does not consider the problem as two separate dualities of value-
output and price-output but links them together. He recognises
explicitly that Marxian theory employs two separate accounting systems
in terms of values and prices since "In the capitalist economy (unlike
the society with simple commodity production) values and prices, in
general, no longer coincide; they should be distinct." (p. 46).

While Morishima sets up his system for many goods, let us set up
a two Department scheme in terms of the λ equations above. Thus the
total values of Department I is λ_1 and of Department II is λ_2 and we
have

$$\lambda_1 = a_{11} \lambda_1 \quad\quad + L_1$$
$$\lambda_2 = a_{12} \lambda_1 \quad\quad + L_2$$

Output of Department II is consumed by workers but does not enter
production as inputs. The technological coefficients a_{11}, a_{12}, L_1

and L_2 determine the values. To quote Morishima, "Values are thus determined socially. But it must be noted that they are determined only by technologicial coefficients, a_{ij}'s and L_i's; they are independent of the market, the class structure of the society, taxes and so on." Morishima, like Samuelson, makes values technologically determinate. (Notice that Samuelson's input-output table can be written as above when combined with his technological equations. Thus b_1 is similar to a_{11} and b_2 to a_{12}. λ_1 is the labour time equivalent of K and λ_2 of Y and so on).

Now the rate of exploitation can be defined in the value domain (λ) and the rate of profit in the price domain (ρ). Morishima begins with the concept of a basket of consumption goods which make up the means of subsistence for the worker. Following the notation used by Samuelson, let us call it $\bar{y}$. Now $\lambda_2\bar{y}$ is labour time embodied in the subsistence basket. The length of the working day is T which must under capitalism be greater than $\lambda_2\bar{y}$; the maximum length of the working day is $\bar{T}$. A measure of the rate of exploitation (r) is

$$r = \frac{T - \lambda_2\bar{y}}{\lambda_2\bar{y}}$$

$(T - \lambda_2\bar{y})$ is the measure of surplus labour since $\lambda_2\bar{y}$ is the exchange value of labour power measured in labour time and T is the length of the working day. Alternative measures can be derived in terms of value of physical quantity of K and Y necessary for providing $\bar{y}$ to all the workers compared to the total value. This can help translate the above equations into Marx's C, V and S (for details see Morishima pp. 48-49).

Actual hourly wage rate w bears a relation to $\bar{y}$. The daily wage income T_w and the price measure of $\bar{y}$ is $p_2\bar{y}$. Now wage rate can be above but not below the value of labour power. Thus $T_w \geqslant p_2\bar{y}$. In order to earn positive profits, Morishima's two price equations can be written as

$$p_1 = (1 + \rho)[p_1 a_{11} + wL_1]$$
$$p_2 = (1 + \rho)[p_2 a_{12} + wL_2]$$

Now what is the relationship between ρ and r? Morishima shows that one can have a positive rate of profit, i.e. $\rho > 0$, only if the rate of exploitation is positive. The rate of exploitation is positive when the hourly real wage rate w/p_2 is at an appropriately low level. Morishima calls this result (due to N. Okishio) "the Fundamental Marxian theorem, because it asserts that the exploitation of labourers by capitalists is necessary and sufficient for the existence of a price-wage set yielding positive profits or, in other words, for the possibility of conserving the capitalist economy" (p.53).

We shall not go into the proof of this theorem here. Morishima derives the exploitation rate curve from the relationship between r and w/p_2 and relates it later to a wage-profit curve. The exploitation rate curve shown below gives a maximum rate of exploitation when the length of the working day is at its maximum and the value of the real wage rate (in terms of labour time) is equal to $1/\bar{T}$ and r is zero when the real wage rate fully absorbs the labour time contained in the working day $\lambda_2\bar{y} = 1$. The actual rate of exploitation depends then upon the forces determining the length of the working day. The actual wage rate can be above subsistence and may involve a wide variety of goods for the workers to choose from; all we need is that the labour time

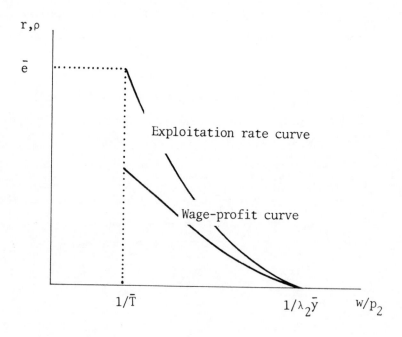

embodied in the worker's consumption basket still leave some surplus labour time and hence a positive rate of exploitation. As wage rate rises above subsistence, the profit wage curve will lie below the exploitation rate curve. The profit rate (ρ) will always be below the rate of exploitation (r) in the Marxian system except when both are zero but these two are inter-related as we showed above in Bortkiewicz's solution (equation (14) above). The rate of profit is below the rate of exploitation because the capitalists buy the materials of production from other capitalists to whom he has to pay their rate of surplus value. If he only employed labour and no constant capital, and was able to keep the wage rate to subsistence level then the rate of profit would equal the rate of exploitation. The relationship between the profit rate, rate of exploitation and the real wage rate is given in the Figure above which reproduces Morishima's Figure 2.

Morishima's treatment of the transformation problem is thus much more detailed and sympathetic compared to Samuelson's treatment. Towards the end of his book, however, Morishima urges the abandonment of the labour theory of value. In a sense, this conclusion of his is similar to the opinion expressed by Joan Robinson in her *Essay on Marxian Economics*. Morishima's reasons are, however, different. The complications are caused, in his opinion, by the durability of capital goods and the heterogeneity of labour with respect to skills. When goods are produced by durable machine goods, at the end of the production period one is left with output in the form of commodity produced and old machine goods which can be re-used. Thus output and old machines are *jointly produced* when machines are durable. This situation was first analysed by von Neumann. Such joint production makes the two Department distinction difficult. The problem of skilled and unskilled labour jointly being used in production also causes accounting difficulty in the value scheme. Morishima maintains that a two-class division of society into workers and capitalists is tenable only if all workers are exploited at the same rate. Now even if one were to reduce skilled labour to unskilled labour by some process of regarding skilled labour as being equal to so many units of unskilled labour, the rates of exploitation of each skill level worker may not equalise. Morishima therefore says "We conclude by suggesting to Marxian economists that they ought radically to change their attitude towards the labour theory of value. If it has to determine the amounts of labour which the techniques of production actually adopted in a capitalist economy require, directly and indirectly, in order to produce commodities, it is not a satisfactory theory at all" (p.193).

Morishima must therefore regard the task of labour theory of value as determining labour allocation over different activities. At the beginning of our discussion of his contribution, we cited him saying that values were determined by technology independent of the class structure of society. He now seeks to abandon the technological value system for what seem to be complications caused by technical problems of durability of capital and heterogeneity of skills. We need, however, to examine more closely Morishima's objections especially regarding the rate of exploitation being unequal when skills are heterogenous.

If the determinants of value systems are purely technological, then indeed a mathematically superior model ought to supersede an old model. But the rate of exploitation in a society is not independent of the class structure or of the relative strength of the classes at any particular moment. We have cited Marx above in saying that the length of the working day is determined by class struggle and, as examples of forms of class struggle, he mentions the revolution of 1848 in France which shortened the working day in all industries and the method of piecemeal legislation in England which reduced it industry by industry ({25}, {27}; for the specific discussion of France and England see the paragraphs following {27} in *Capital*, Vol. I). Indeed Morishima himself recognises this in his discussion of the rate of exploitation where he says, "So the problem of determining the rate of exploitation is reduced to the problem of determining the length of the working day. When the worker's position is very weak, the working day will be maximised..." (p.55).

Now in the course of uneven development of the class struggle in different industries and in different countries, the length of the working day can differ and so can the rate of exploitation. Equal rates of exploitation across industries were assumed by Marx to make the arithmetic of the value-price problem simple. It is not a necessary part of Marxian model except in making the transformation problem soluble. Marxist historians have pointed out that even within the working class there may be group of aristocratic labourers who are better off than their fellow workers. The uniformity of rate of exploitation is incompatible with an historical model since in actual life the uneven development of capitalism and of the class struggle leads to uneven rates of exploitation. Skilled labour in some industries unionise earlier and grows stronger than unskilled labour; some superior skilled persons - professions, civil servants - have unionises only in recent years. The length of the working day is often different in different industries and so is the wage rate. If the introduction of skilled labour leads to unequal rate of exploitation in our model, so be it. A mathematical difficulty should not prevent us from trying to use and extend the model so that it approximates the historical situation.

Being isolated from the historical dimension of the class struggle, Morishima's interpretation of Marx remains partial. We agree with him that as a theory of allocation of resources, the labour theory of value should be abandoned, but it was never meant for such an operational task.

Morishima's discussion however does point out that any extension of the value-price problem beyond its present academic stage must furnish a theory of two aspects. One is the determinants of the length of the working day. Historical quantitative studies are necessary to put flesh into the notion of the class struggle being the determining factor. Marx's discussion of the working day in *Capital*, Vol. I, gives many instances but more needs to be done. The second aspect is the gap between the real wage rate and the exchange value of labour power. Once again growth of trade unions, international migration of labour and capital, rate of technical change, etc., have determined this gap. But a Marxian model needs to be developed here.

The publication of Sraffa's *Production of Commodities by Means of Commodities* has revived interest in the classical labour theory. Sraffa's own concern is with the Ricardian problem of obtaining an invariant measure of value. He also sets up a physical system of commodity and labour inputs which generates a consistent system of outputs, values, wages and profit. The economy he studies can be described by a set of linear equations and involves no change in the scale of operations. It assumes constant technology, abstracts from problems of money and of prices. Sraffa's model has generated a tremendous interest among economists interested in the Marxian system and many have seen the model as the best formulation of the Marxian value price problem.

There are many aspects of Sraffa's system which are interesting and in the realm of economic theory revolutionary. As a critique of marginalist theory and especially of capital theory, it has already led to a celebrated debate. Our concern is not with this aspect of Sraffa's system. It is with Sraffa's model as a tool for analysis in Marxian economic theory.

Sraffa himself has not addressed himself to the Marxian value price problem at all. It is his modern formulation of the labour theory of value, his complete break with the Neoclassical tradition and the similarities between his system of equations and the Marxian system which has led scholars such as Dobb and Meek among others to suggest that his system should form the basis of Marxian economic theory.

The structure of Sraffa's system in its mathematical details is fairly similar to Morishima's models. Unlike Morishima, Sraffa does not have a value system, a physical system and a price system. Physical quantities of inputs are multiplied by their prices (or what Sraffa calls values). This expression then gives the total material costs of production upon which a rate of profit is applied. Adding labour costs to this sum gives the value of output or total revenue. To write the system in Sraffa's notation for two commodities A and B we have

$$Ap_a = (A_a p_a + B_a p_b)(1 + \rho) + L_a W$$
$$Bp_b = (A_b p_a + B_b p_b)(1 + \rho) + L_b W$$

Sraffa's assumption is that wages are not advanced but paid at the end of the production period hence they do not get multiplied by the rate of profit. A_a is the amount of A used in the production of A, B_a the amount of B used in the production of B. p_a and p_b are the prices of A and B. ρ is the rate of profit (Sraffa labels it r but we have re-labelled it here to conform to earlier notation). w is the wage per unit of labour and L_a and L_b are the labour inputs. The similarity of this system to Morishima's is in the coefficients A_a, A_b etc. The difference is in applying the rate of profit to material input alone but not to the labour input. Thus it is not a conventional ρ mark-up pricing equations system. We have further conditions that output of each commodity is at least as large as its use as input $A_a + A_b < A$, $B_a + B_b < B$ and for convention $L_a + L_b = 1$. National income can also be defined in the system as price times the excess of output over inputs

$$[A - (A_a + A_b)]p_a + [B - (B_a + B_b)]p_b$$

We have three equations now and four unknowns p_a, p_b, w, ρ.

In exploring the relationship between the rate of profit ρ and the wage rate w, Sraffa employs the notion of a wage-profit curve similar to Morishima's. As in the Marx-Bortkiewitz solutions, the (price) rate of profit ρ and the (value) rate of profit $(\bar{p})$ diverge in a world of more than one commodity. The rate of profit ρ also diverges from the rate of surplus value (r). Sraffa brings out this divergence by saying that while an equal rate of profit ρ is earned in every industry, the value measure of the net product to the means of production differs in different industries. Only when wages are zero and the rate of profit is at its maximum do these two measures coincide. The wage profit frontier then traces out the rate of profit consistent with each level of wage rate given the technological coefficients. As in the Morishima diagram, when the wage rate is at maximum, the profit rate is zero. If ρ_{max} is the maximum rate of profit, Sraffa's formula is

$$\rho = \rho_{max} (1 - w)$$

A wage-profit frontier such as derived by Morishima and Sraffa from slightly different models can be easily misunderstood as an analytical formulation of the notion of class struggle. What could make the two class divisions and the antagonism between the classes clearer than such a frontier, it may be said. It is necessary therefore to examine the usefulness of the wage-profit frontier in analysing economic reality. We begin by assuming that regardless of the level of profit rate or wage rate, the technology as embodied in the input-output co-efficients is unaffected. At any point of time, an economy is on one point on the curve. If the wage rate were to change, realistically the technology would change in an attempt on the part of the capitalists to maintain the rate of profit. But then with a changed technology, we will get a new wage-profit curve altogether. It is not possible to travel up and down the wage-profit curve. The wage-profit curve cannot therefore throw any light on an historical phenomenon, a phenomenon taking place over time such as the class struggle. It remains an esoteric tool to clarify certain logical puzzles in economic theory; it is of no help in studying social relations.

Modern interpretations of Marx whether by economists hostile to his ideas or by his champions, seem to rely on a technological deter-minism based on a physical input-output system. This is reinforced by mechanistic assumptions about the determinants of the wage rate - in most cases a constant subsistence wage rate tends to be assumed. Having thus shorn Marxian theory of its historical and social content, having stripped it of its qualitative dynamics, an emasculated version of his model is retained to be criticised or worshipped, but not to be used as a tool for advancing our understanding of the real world. It is only in such emasculated systems that rising real wages and standards of living, shortening hours of work, continuous full employment etc. are seen as embarrassing to the Marxian model, to be regarded by the critics as refutations and to be denounced by the champions as illusory.

All this is not said in a diehard defence of Marx's model. Whether we accept his theory or reject it, we need to specify correctly and com-pletely all the aspects of his model. We cannot neglect some aspects as 'sociological' and then discard the remaining bits of the concept of value as mystical. By neglecting the qualitative aspects of class relations, we merely reduce the Marxian schema to a Ricardian, a Leontieff or a von-Neumann schema. Interesting as these schema are, their acceptance or rejection throws little light on the Marxian model.

While Marx began with simple reproduction, he always emphasised that it was in the nature of capitalism to change - to revolutionise values constantly. It is therefore necessary to move on to a discussion of *expanded reproduction*. Unlike the transformation problem, very little attention has been paid to Marx's discussion of expanded reproduction. Such attention as has been paid by economists has acknowledged the pioneering efforts of Marx in this area, but there has been little critical discussion of the logic of the expanded reproduction scheme. Marx himself discussed expanded reproduction in detail only in the concluding chapters of Vol. II of *Capital*. It was left to Rosa Luxemburg to raise many questions about expanded reproduction which are as yet not fully answered. These questions will form our main concern in the next chapter and will point to many areas of research in this field.

THE MARXIAN VALUE-PRICE DUALITY

Invisible Value Domain	Visible Price or Exchange Domain
Social relations between men	Relations between things
Class division between capitalist as owner of means of production and means of subsistence and worker as free labourer	Equal relation of exchange between buyer and seller
Value of labour power equal to the socially necessary labour time required for production and reproduction of the labourer equal to paid labour which is less than total labour expended	The wage form Wages are paid for a full day's work
Rate of surplus value equals $\dfrac{\text{unpaid labour}}{\text{paid labour}}$	Rate of profit $=\dfrac{\text{Profits}}{\text{Stock of fixed capital} + \text{advanced circulating capital}}$
Total value $=$ Surplus value + variable capital + constant capital $=$ (1 + rate of surplus value × variable capital + constant capital, where constant capital has its full value transferred to the final product but creates no surplus value	Total profits $=$ Total revenue minus total cost $=$ Selling price minus cost price. where cost price equals cost of labour (wage bill) plus cost of materials and wear and tear of fixed capital

XIII

EXTENDED REPRODUCTION: INTRODUCTION

At many points in all the three volumes of *Capital*, Marx emphasises that a revolution in value takes place continuously within the
productive process under capitalism {34} {47} {68}. Changing technology as well as improvements in methods of utilizing given inputs,
revolution in methods of circulation (packaging, transport, credit,
marketing) are all occurring all the time. Along with growth and as
a necessary part of it are crises - business cycles which force change
upon individual capitalists {75}. In addition to these is the course
of the class struggle - strikes, trade union growth, growth of new
forms of capitalist associations e.g. multinational firms, changes in
form of governments, e.g. growth of the welfare state etc. Beyond
mentioning these changes, we can do little more because these have not
been treated in analytical detail to any great extent. Historians
have charted many of these changes with great success but economists
have failed to incorporate them in their formal schemes.

In Marx's own discussions, there is a contrast between his arithmetical examples of expanded reproduction and his many discussions in
the 'literary' parts. The arithmetical examples - the 'model' of
extended reproduction - is constructed so as to show a *balanced* and
continuous growth of the two Departments under fairly restrictive
assumptions. It is when we come to look at the logic behind such
balanced growth that several contradictions emerge. Once again the
unsolved problems are those of prices and of the money circuit. But
let us first set out Marx's model.

Chapter XXI of Vol. II of *Capital* is devoted to "Accumulation and
Reproduction in an Extended Scale." Marx's examples are constructed

with a two Department scheme as in our equations (1) under Simple Repr-
duction. Marx further imposes two assumptions which are in no way a
necessary part of his theory but convenient for arithmetical calculations.[1] These are (1) identical rates of exploitation in the two
Departments (r_i = r) which also remains *constant* throughout accumulati
(r_{it} = r_i = r); (2) given values of organic compositions for the two
Departments which also remain *constant* throughout accumulation. The
rate of exploitation was assumed to be 100 percent. In Department I,
the organic composition was 4/5 and in Department II 2/3. All the
discussion is throughout carried out in terms of values rather than
(i.e. proportional to) prices. (It was not until Vol. III that Marx
came to the value-price transformation problem).

In order to satisfy the two assumptions, Marx further assumed
that one half of surplus value of Department I - the machine goods
producing Department - is reinvested or readvanced as capital and the
remainder is spent on wage goods. This makes the activities of the
capitalists of Department II completely dependent on what Department I
does and on the balancing equations required to ensure that all the
assumptions are fulfilled. (This has often led to a general policy
of the 'primacy' of Department I in Soviet Union and Eastern European
countries. It is necessary, therefore, to emphasise that this assumption is for *arithmetical* convenience and not required for the general
model).

Marx's tables for expanded reproduction are given in Table III.
We see that r = 100% and g_1 = 4/5, g_2 = 2/3. Total output of Department I is 6,000 whereas the total demand for C_i as input is only 5500.
Thus $Y_1 > C_1$. By analogy we have V + S = 3500 whereas the output of
Department II is only 3000. Remember that since we do not have Depart
ment III, surplus value must be spent either on Department I or Depart
ment II, unlike in the three Department representation of simple repro
duction. The discrepancy between Y_1 and C and Y_2 and S + V clearly
indicates that the system is not in simple reproduction. The capitali
do not spend all their surplus value as revenue but advance it as capi
The simple rule is that $\frac{1}{2}$ of S_1 - surplus value in Department I- is accu
lated as capital. In order to preserve the organic composition g_1 at
4/5, only 4/5 of $\frac{1}{2}$ of S_1 is advanced as constant capital. Thus out of

S_1 of 1000, 400 is advanced as constant capital, 100 as variable capital and 500 as spent as revenue on goods of Department II.

This arbitrary rule for Department I capitalists completely closes the system since we then impose the balancing identities that *ex post* $Y_1 = C$ and $Y_2 = S + V$. The *ex post* C, V, S are different from the initial or *ex ante* categories. They are what would appear as final expenditure (in value terms). Thus S in the *ex post* scheme is not total surplus value but the value of capitalists' purchase of wage goods. In price terms or in value terms, the *ex post* S is not identifiable with surplus value nor useful as a measure of exploitation. (We shall return to this extremely important point later. Suffice it to say now that this distinction has important bearing on Baran and Sweezy's critique of the law of falling rate of profit and their new law of rising surplus).

Given Department I's decision and the identities, Department II makes up the gap in this scheme. Let us denote the *ex ante* categories by asterisks, remembering as always that they are not directly observable. Then the *ex post* $C_1 = C_1^* + \frac{1}{2}g_1 S_1^*$ and $C_2 = Y_1 - C_1$. Thus though $Y_1^* > C^*$, $Y_1 = C$. Given C_2 it is easy to see that Y_2 is determined by g_2 — the organic composition has to be maintained at 2/3. Thus we get $C_2 - C_2^*$ and $V_2 - V_2^*$ as the net accumulation out of S_2^* by Department II, the remainder being spent as revenue on wage goods.

TABLE III

Numerical Examples of Extended Reproduction

Year		C_i	V_i	S_i	Y_i	
1	Dept. I	4000	1000	1000	6000	) Initial Scheme for Year 1
	Dept II	1500	750	750	3000	*Ex ante*
		5500	1750	1750	9000	
2	Dept. I	4400	1100	500	6000	) "Arrangement changed for the purposes of accumulation"
	Dept. II	1600	800	600	3000	
		6000	1900	1100	9000	*Ex Post* Scheme for Year 2

TABLE III contd.

Dept. I	4400	1100	1100	6600	Initial Scheme for Year
Dept. II	1600	800	800	3200	
	6000	1900	1900	9800	
Dept. I	4840	1210	550	6600	*Ex Post* Scheme for Year
Dept. II	1760	880	560	3200	
	6600	2090	1110	9800	
Dept. I	4840	1210	1210	7260	Initial Scheme for Year
Dept. II	1760	880	880	3520	
	6600	2090	2090	10780	
Dept. I	5324	1331	605	7260	*Ex Post* Scheme for Year
Dept. II	1936	968	616	3520	
	7260	2299	1221	10780	
Dept. I	5324	1331	1331	7986	Initial Scheme for Year
Dept. II	1936	968	968	3872	
	7260	2299	2299	11858	
Dept. I	5856	1464	666	7986	*Ex Post* Scheme for Year
Dept. II	2129	1065	677	3872	
	7985	2529	1344	11858	
Dept. I	5856	1464	1464	8784	Initial Scheme for Year
Dept. II	2129	1065	1065	4259	
	7985	2529	2529	13043	
Dept. I	6442	1610	732	8784	*Ex Post* Scheme for Year
Dept. II	2342	1172	745	4259	
	8784	2782	1477	13043	
Dept. I	6442	1610	1610	9662	Initial Scheme for Year
Dept. II	2342	1172	1172	4686	
	8784	2782	2782	14348	

The decision to accumulate has its own consequences however. Now the capitalists of Department I have advanced 4400 C_1 and 1100 V_1 which when put into production as productive capital generate surplus value of 1100 and at the end of the productive process given total value of 6600. Similarly Department II has total output of 3200 since the advanced capital is 1600 + 800. Thus whereas the *ex post* expenditures in Year 1 add up to -absorb - total value produced, this implies a similar *ex ante* imbalance for Year 2. Once again $Y_1^* > C^*$ and $Y_2^* < (V^* + S^*)$. Once again the decision by Department I capitalists to accumulate $\frac{1}{2}$ of S_1^* will yield numbers which *ex post* will satisfy the balancing equations.

Before we look critically at the process by which *ex post* harmony is established from *ex ante* conditions of disequilibrium, let us examine the quantitative dimensions of the solution (Table IV). The total value output goes up from 6000 to 14,348 by the sixth year. This involves, apart from the first year when the growth rate is 9%, a steady growth rate of 10% per year. The value of machine goods output grows steadily at 10% per annum. The value rate of profit ($\bar{p}$ in our notation) is constant at 24%. Given the equal rate of exploitation and the unequal organic composition of capital, *the value rate of profit in one Department is different from that in the other*. The expenditure of Department I capitalist on wage goods goes up every year by 10% (in value terms). It is the expenditure of Department II capitalists on wage goods and by implication their rate of accumulation which changes from one year to the next. We see in Table IV that the expenditure on wage goods for Department II capitalists goes from 600, 560, 616, 678, 745.... It is only after the second year that it grows at 10%; for the first year it goes down by about 6%.

While not much emphasis should be put on actual magnitudes in this example, it raises very important questions. We have in this example a capitalist economy capable of growing at 10% for ever and ever, with the value rate of profit constant and no upward tendency in the overall organic composition of capital. Is this example to illustrate the possibility of a crisis free growth of capitalism or is it designed to show how unlikely it is that so many balancing conditions will be simultaneously satisfied? What is the mechanism that ensures that these conditions will be fulfilled year after year?

TABLE IV

Expanded Reproduction: A Summary View

	Total Value of output	Change in Value of Output	Value of Machine Goods Output	Change in Value of Output	Value Rate of Profit	Capitalist Spending on Wage Goods	
	$Y_1 + Y_2$	$\Delta(Y_1 + Y_2)$	Y_1	ΔY_1	$S^*/C^* + V^*$	Dept.I	Dept
1	9000		6000			500	600
2	9800	800(9%)	6600	600 (10%)	1750/7250 = 24	605	560
3	10780	980(10%)	7260	660 (10%)	1900/7900 = 24	605	610
4	11858	1078(10%)	7986	726 (10%)	2090/8690 = 24	666	678
5	13043	1185(10%)	8784	798 (10%)	2299/9559 = 24	732	745
6	14348	1304(10%)	9662	878 (10%)	2529/10514= 24		

The arbitrariness of the rule by which Department I capitalists invest half their surplus value has already been mentioned. Notice also that they reinvest only within their industry; all investment is internally financed. What guides them to decide on these matters? Is it the desire to maintain a certain money rate of profit or to bridge the gap between the money rate of profit in the two sectors? We need to know the prices corresponding to the values and the money rate of profit each year to be able to know the *process* by which profits are equalised and prices set. It *may* be that at the level of prices, the equilibrium growth pattern of value sums is disturbed. Marx clearly has failed to pose the problem of expanded reproduction in the price domain. He also does not explicitly solve the problem of expanded reproduction in the M - M' circuit. His attempts to introduce monetary circulation in this scheme are incomplete and unsatisfactory. This indeed is at the heart of Rosa Luxemburg's critique of Marx's scheme.[2]

Rosa Luxemburg rejects the picture of balanced capitalist growth as unrealistic. Fluctuations in the rate of growth from one year to the next and the uneven growth of one Department as compared to the other are for her the main features of capitalism. Marx's model cannot explain cyclical growth and crises of accumulation. In fact, the model contradicts Marx's position in Vols. I and III of *Capital*. Marx saw the capitalist system as ridden by "the inherent contradiction between the unlimited expansive capacity of the productive forces and the limited expansive capacity of social consumption under conditions of capitalist distribution." The tendency of the rate of profit to fall, for the organic composition of capital to rise, for the reserve army of labour to swell - all these have no place in the scheme of expanded reproduction as outlined by Marx in Vol. II of *Capital* and summarised above. If it only needs ·a decision by capitalists of Department I to invest half of their surplus value every year, there should be no problem in sustaining balanced growth. Clearly something has gone wrong.

XIV

ROSA LUXEMBURG'S CRITIQUE

Rosa Luxemburg starts with the question of the incentive in the system to expand at 10% per annum. Why should Department I expand at 10%? Why should the capitalists decide to accumulate? The question of technical change - revolution in methods of production continuously changing values forcing capitalists to accumulate in order to keep up with competitors - has been ignored by Marx in this discussion. The value sums grow at given rates due to accumulation of surplus value rather than due to technical change. What is the driving force then for accumulation?

We begin with the initial situation where we have already left simple reproduction behind. There is clearly excess value of machine goods output being produced in relation to its rate of use. Where will the extra demand come from for 500 value units of machine goods? According to Marx, the capitalists of Department I decide to demand 400 units for themselves. They decide for some reason to expand. Being rational, they must do this with some expectations of rising demand for their product in the future although at the moment they face a demand gap. If we grant that they invest 400 they still need to spend 100 on variable capital. They cannot however pay their workers - both old and new - in machine goods. They must sell their entire output 6000 (or of 1600 deducting 4400 for their own use), convert it into money and then go out into the market for more workers. In terms of the three circuits of capital, they have to go through the $C' - M' \to C$ circuit. They can sell their output and convert it into money and advance 100 additional value units as variable capital and spend 500 units on wage goods only if there is a market for them. This market

84

in the arithmetical scheme is provided by Department II. Quite arbitrarily, Department II decides to mop up all the excess supply of machine goods 1500 + 100 so that Department I can grow at 10%. In the process they, too, have to sell their entire output of 3000. *Ex ante* if the capitalists of Department I do not take into their heads to accumulate as much as $\frac{1}{2}$ of their surplus value, Department II faces a happy situation of excess demand (in value terms) for their product. But still they must sell their product before they can buy 100 additional value units of machine goods from Department I. What guarantees the mutual sale? Where does Department I get *the money* to buy 100 units of constant capital?

A hoard of money from previous years was tentatively suggested by Marx as the answer. This hoard of money may consist of accumulated unspent parts of m, e.g. in depreciation reserve. The problem is however not of some past hoard but of expected future demand. Why does Department I want to expand at all, even if it could find the money to finance purchase of 100 units of variable capital? It cannot be for the capitalists' consumption since their consumption could be higher without growth; in any case, the driving force of capitalism for Marx is not capitalists' consumption but profits. It cannot be that it is the workers' growing demand which drives accumulation; workers can have no demand for wage goods unless they are employed and their continued employment depends on accumulation and not vice versa. "This means that the starting point of capitalist production is not a given number of workers and their demands, but that these factors themselves are constantly fluctuating; dependent variables of the capitalists' expectations of profit."[1]

Growing population either of the capitalists or of the workers by the same logic cannot provide an explanation for growth. The existence of a 'middle class' of rentiers, clergy, government officials, teachers is rejected by Marx as a possible source for demand since these derive their income from surplus value and cannot have demand over and above what is already present in capitalist spending on wage goods. (The 'third' class or the third Department is however an important escape hatch in recent debates among Marxists about the remarkable capacity of capitalism to survive and expand. We shall

85

discuss this later). Marx also rejects the idea of foreign trade - dumping surplus output in other capitalist countries. This can have only relevance for a country but, taking the capitalist system as a whole, the problem remains.[2] (It should be added, however, that despite this rejection the importance of international trade for capitalists of one country as a solution for their own crises is quite obvious. Many of the post Second World War crises in the sphere of international trade and payments arise out of the successful attempts of some countries to solve their accumulation problem in foreign trade as against their less successful rivals).

The puzzle therefore remains. In the scheme for expanded reproduction, capitalists of both Departments miraculously seem to be able to realize surplus and total value by selling to each other for ever and ever. There is no realisation problem, no monetary crisis, no brake on accumulation. This contradicts Marx's own emphasis on the inherent contradictions of capitalism. It is this contradiction between the picture of capitalism ridden by crises and faced with a long run tendency of the rate of profit to fall in Vol. III and the smooth expansion of Volume II which is *the central unsolved problem of Marxian dynamics*. It is of much greater importance then the value-price contradiction of Vol. I and Vol. III - the transformation problem which has been much discussed by economists from Bohm Bawerk onwards.

There was an intense debate among Russian Marxists during the 1890's regarding this problem. A large section of Rosa Luxemburg's work is devoted to this debate in which Tugan-Baranowsky, Lenin and many of the leading Russian Narodniks and legal Marxists participated. They did not however advance the problem beyond where Marx had left it. Rosa Luxemburg in the last section of her book advances her own solution to this problem. We shall devote the next section to her solution and then return to take another look at why the problem arises.

XV

ROSA LUXEMBURG'S SOLUTION [1]

Rosa Luxemburg's solution is to place capitalist expansion in a realistic social context where it is surrounded by non-capitalist (pre-capitalist) modes of production. Instead of assuming as Marx did for the theoretical model that the capitalist mode was universally prevalent, she argues that a capitalist mode emerges from a pre-capitalist setting at home and has access to pre-capitalist countries abroad as well. 19th century trade and imperialism are the more realistic setting for the expansion of capitalism in the 19th century and she incorporates these into the model of expanded reproduction.

Her analysis, though not formal, is quite detailed. She cites the sale of British cotton textiles (Department II) to foreign markets such as India and the export of British railroad equipment (Department I) to European countries and USA as examples whereby internationaltrade within the capitalist world, but especially with the outside non-capitalist world, helps realise value, particularly surplus value. The access to increasing raw materials as constant capital for expanding reproduction is provided by increasing productivity in the use of existing materials from Nature and from the non-capitalist countries themselves. Many consumer goods and means of production are also produced outside the capitalist system - import of corn into Britain from Russia. International trade thus helps to realise surplus value and, by acquiring raw materials from abroad, to generate further surplus value.

Where does the labour power necessary for expanded reproduction come from? The amount of variable capital goes on expanding each year in line with expansion of capital but this requires additional labour power to be on hand. Here again, Rosa Luxemburg mentions the decay of pre-capitalist sectors - artisans, agricultural labourers, international migration from non-capitalist countries (Irish migration to the US). This shows the dependence of the capitalist sector on the non-capitalist. By access to non-capitalist markets and sources of supply Rosa Luxemburg sees capitalism as transforming the non-capitalist world in its own image. Commodity exchange is introduced, with private property in land and natural resources and conditions of wage labour in the non-capitalist world. So contradictions are present even in the search for an escape from contradictions.

With respect to trade with other capitalist countries, especially those struggling to emerge into capitalist status, Rosa Luxemburg emphasises the role of international loans - private capital flows abroad. These help finance the purchase of the surplus product of the lending country and retain its influence on these newly emerging countries. The *surplus value is then realised* from the peasants and proletariat of the borrowing country be it pre-capitalist or newly capitalist. The smooth expansion of the old country is financed then partly from a tax on the peasants of the new country.

Lastly, Rosa Luxemburg mentions militarism as a factor. Here she introduces a third Department which makes armaments. As a starting point 100 units of variable capital are diverted away from the workers by providing them fewer means of subsistence, e.g. forced saving by inflation. This leads to a diminution of the aggregate social product (output of Departments I and II) but this diminution need not diminish the total surplus value according to her model. The diminution in the aggregate social product can come out of diminution of constant capital and a decline in the variable capital. The formal details of this three Department model are worth setting out.

Taking as her example a different illustration of expanded repro-- duction than the one we have discussed above (also taken from Vol. II of *Capital*), the model is as follows

	C_i	V_i	S_i		
I	5000	1000	1000	7000	
II	1430	285	285	2000	Initial Scheme
	6430	1285	1285	9000	

Now suppose that workers receive only 1185 units of value in means of subsistence and the 100 is diverted to armaments. The armaments industry has the same organic composition as the two Departments 5/6 and 100% rate of exploitation. Thus we have in this Department III

$$71.5 + 14.25 + 14.25 = 100$$

But this reduction of 100 in demand for means of subsistence alters all the amounts in Departments I and II. We get finally

	c_i	v_i	s_i	
I	4949	989.75	989.75	6928.5
II	1358.5	270.75	270.75	1900
	6307.5	1260.50	1260.50	8828.5

There is no reason however for the decline in surplus value since only the upkeep of the workers has reduced in value. The entire drop in the aggregate social product equal to the 171.5 drop in aggregate social product must come off the variable capital if possible rather than from surplus value. A drop of 171.5 in aggregate variable capital could lead finally to the following composition for the aggregate product

$$6430C + 1113.5V + 1285S = 8828.5$$

If the adjustment were to come from constant capital instead of variable capital, we could get

$$6307.5C + 1236V + 1285S = 8828.5$$

The effect of armaments cut then is to reduce aggregate social product but while the value of armaments output does not enter the aggregate social product as Marx defines it, it still represents a market for selling of output of Departments I and II. From the point of view of the *individual* capitalists, there is no change since the market for 100 means of subsistence is replaced by that of 100 armaments. Armaments

89

do not need to be sold on the market since they are paid for by taxa-
tion but the armaments sector purchases inputs from the other Departments.

If the drop in variable capital has been financed by inflation,
then prices of all goods would be higher though not by the same proportion as a result of this diversion. Adding the 100 units of armaments
to 8828.5 (as in the current practice in national income accounting)
we get 9928.5 value units of national income. We still have to derive
money value of output since we *may* get a higher money value of output
as a result.

This point has a bearing on the question of fiscal policy multi-
pliers. The multiplier of 100 units of armaments financed by 100 taxa-
tion may be greater than one if we follow the modern rather than the
Marxian national income accounting. We shall take up this problem
when discussing the impact of Keynes in modern Marxian economics. This
does however point to a major flaw in Marx and Rosa Luxemburg's analysis of the problem of expanded reproduction. This is their failure to
check the price consequences of expanded reproduction. By posing the
problem in value terms alone, they fail to explore fully the process
by which realization problems are met under commodity exchange. This
is not an easy problem to solve but we shall indicate in the next
Chapter the direction in which the answer may be found.

EXPANDED REPRODUCTION: ADDITIONAL CONSIDERATIONS

The dual relation between values and prices much emphasised in
the beginning of Vol. I of *Capital*, and of such importance in the transformation problem, is not mentioned by Marx explicitly in Vol. II
during his discussion of expanded reproduction. As we know from
Bortkiewicz's solution, the value rate of profit and the money rate
of profit can diverge systematically. The problem of translating
values to prices and vice versa is quite challenging in simple reproduction. Clearly it cannot be ignored at this stage. This is not just
because of the fascination of a logical exercise. The crises of the
capitalist economy take place within the domain of exchange - prices
fall, excess supply appears, credit shrinks, firms go bankrupt, unem-
ployment rises etc. during a slump. While the structural model explaining crises is in terms of value relations - rate of exploitation,
organic composition of capital, the class division, the manifestation
of these crises is in terms of price relations.

A theory of crises in terms of price relations as well as value
relations is absolutely essential because the behaviour of capitalists
and workers is in terms of prices, profits, wages, cost-price ratios
etc. This may seem to contradict our earlier characterization of value
relations as structural equations but this is not so. Value relations
are not *behavioural equations* in the sense in which in Neoclassical
economic theory one talks of behavioural relations. Value relations
are not perceived by individual participants in the economic process.
Only the political economi t, as a scientist, discovers the value
relations underlying the apparent behavioural relations. This is
Marx's view of science. Marx attacked 'vulgar economy' for failing to

go beyond the apparent. To quote Marx directly: "All science would be superfluous if the outward appearance and the essence of things directly coincided."[1]

The decision to invest one half of surplus value of Department I in order for the economy to grow at a sustained rate is a solution to the problems of accumulation crises only to the 'planner' or to the political economist. This is because he models the economy in the essential value relations not in behavioural equations. For an individual capitalist, however, the notion of balanced growth is of little relevance; he makes his decisions so as to get maximum profits. Capital moves from one firm to another or from one industry to another seeking the highest rate of return, thus equalising the rate of profit across industries. Marx is much concerned with this problem when setting out the three circuits of capital. Indeed the circuit of money capital is important because once commodity capital has been converted into money then capital exists in its 'natural form' and can be re-invested anywhere or spent as revenue. The decision of Department I to invest one half of its surplus value must be rationalised in terms of the movement of prices and profit.

Even at the aggregate level, if we are to study the consequences of departure from balanced growth - say due to a rise in the rate of exploitation in one Department relative to another - these can only be studied in terms of national income data. Thus the amount of surplus value spent on wage goods plus the amount advanced as variable capital will appear as total consumers' expenditure in price terms. In discussing the role of the armaments sector, we observe that while according to Marx's definitions a diversion of 100 units reduced aggregate social capital by 171 units, this need not appear to be so in national income data. It will only be a reduction of 71 at the most since 100 output of armaments will be added as national income. The actual recorded figure will depend further on relative price movements and the accuracy of the price deflators. It is quite likely that instead of a value 'multiplier' of - 1.7, we may have a positive multiplier in price terms. Let us therefore explore the likely price consequences of expanded reproduction.

Let us begin by looking at the realisation problem. If Table III represented simple reproduction, the capitalists in Department I could realise only 5500 value units rather than 6000 - a shortfall of 1/12. Thus in the C' - M' conversion we should find that *if prices are unchanged* (M' - M) would be 1/12 the smaller than otherwise. One way of selling all the goods would be to reduce the price but this would sell all the C' but M' may still show a short fall. A short fall in M' compared to expectations will lead to a fall in the realised rate of profit and capitalists may convert M' into C not in Department I but in Department II. Department II can realise its total value if at least 1250 out of 1750 (5/7) is spent on wage goods out of surplus value. If not, then the C' - M' conversion in Department II will also show a short fall. A short fall in both the Departments will mean that the total realised value may be much smaller than 9000.

The crucial question then is how is surplus value disposed of by the capitalist? Economists have dealt with this problem - the problem of the investment schedule - in various ways. Marx assumed a co-efficient of $\frac{1}{2}$ for net accumulation in Department I with Department II[I] left to adjust itself. In many growth models set up in terms of price categories or physical input-output categories, it is customary to assume either that all the income of capitalists is saved or that a constant proportion of all income of capitalists and workers is saved and in both these cases automatically invested. More complicated schemes have relied on saving and investment decisions depending on the yield-rate of profit - on different assets. In a Marxian model we are interested in these matters not in order to 'predict' the amount saved or invested. We are not primarily interested in the distribution of surplus value among the capitalists or into the categories of rent, interest, dividends etc. The model of expanded reproduction should help us tie together the disequilibrium (uneven) development of capitalism and the consequential influence on (or rather its dialectical relation with) the growth of class relations. The model if properly developed should explain contemporary capitalism.

We can indicate at this stage the link between prices and values in the model of expanded reproduction. A full solution must await further study but a beginning can be made along the lines of Bortkiewicz's work. For each of the two Departments we can write down the costs and revenue equations as in (10a) and (10b) above. Remember now that the total value produced by, say, Department I (Y_1) is different from total value of constant capital consumed in the production process $C_1 + C_2 = $ So we have

$$p_1 Y_1 = (1 + \rho)(p_1 C_1 + p_2 V_1) \tag{15a}$$
$$p_2 Y_2 = (1 + \rho)(p_2 C_2 + p_2 V_2) \tag{15b}$$

The crucial equation is the total value identity. If we write it as Bortkiewicz does for simple reproduction, we implicitly assume that all surplus value is either invested or consumed. We may then write, instead of (11),

$$p_1 Y_1 + p_2 Y_2 = C + V + S \tag{16}$$

Given (16), prices depend only upon the different organic compositions of capital in the two Departments since the rate of exploitation is by assumption identical and constant. By using equation (7) and the quantities in Table II we get

$$6/5\ p_1 = (1 + \rho)(4/5 p_1 + 1/5 p_2)$$
$$4/3\ p_2 = (1 + \rho)(2/3 p_1 + 1/3 p_2) \tag{17}$$
$$2 p_1 + p_2 + 3$$

Solving p_2 in terms of p_1 as $p_2 = 3 - 2p_1$, we can solve for $(1 + \rho)$ and p_1. Putting $(1 + \rho) = \lambda$ we get an equation

$$\lambda^2 - 11\lambda + 12 = 0$$

Solving it, we get $\lambda = (1 + \rho) = 1.2$ (approximately) as one of the solutions. p_1 is then 1.05 and $p_2 = 0.9$. Thus treating the expanded reproduction system as an analogue of the simple reproduction system, we get a profit rate of 20%, $p_1 = 1.05$ and $p_2 = 0.9$. But this is clearly not going to be of much help in examining the dynamics of the problem because *equation (16) assumes away all the realisation problems*. It is a sort of Say's law! Repeating this exercise for each year's initial scheme will not get us any marked change in p_1, P_2 or ρ. We will travel smoothly along equilibrium path with nearly constant prices. This is because once we assume away the realisation problem, the determinants of prices are the rate of exploitation r and the organic composition of capital in each Department - g_i. The only change in relative prices will come about because the proportion of Y_1 to Y_2 is not strictly 2: 1 throughout but 3.3: 1.6 in year 2 and 3.63: 1.76 in year 3 and so on. This changes the numbers in equation (16) but not by much.

A much more helpful way of tackling this problem is to see that since there is no Department III (and hence no p_3), surplus value must either take the form of machine goods or of wage goods. In Marx's words this is the material form of surplus value as against its value form or its money form. Now the output of Department I being machine goods, value in Department I must be realised by selling all the units of output. No amount of luxury consumption by the capitalist or even doubling wages of workers can alter the fact that 500 more *value* units of machine goods (and equivalent number of machines) are produced than are required to maintain the system in simple reproduction (as productive capital), the system must expand in order to use up these machines. What does not take the form of machine goods tautologically takes the form of wage goods.

Let us look at the process at the level of exchange. There is an excess supply of machine goods and excess demand for wage goods if the system is in simple reproduction (i.e. all surplus value spent on wage goods). The price of wage goods should rise relatively to that of machine goods. This leads the capitalists in Department II to expand their production. Any decision by them to expand means demand for machine goods and wage goods as capital. Investment of this expected profit will lead to a diminution in the amount of surplus value left for spending on wage goods - the diminution being exactly equal to the additional amount invested as constant capital. The price gap will thus narrow in favour of Department I. In order to provide the additional amount of machines to Department II *now and in the future*, the capitalists of Department I step up their own rate of output. The gap between prices and between profit rates thus narrows, bringing the system into *ex post* equilibrium. The expansion of the system however depends upon future sustained growth and there is always an *ex ante* disequilibrium due to this.

This is not the way either Marx or Rosa Luxemburg tackled this problem. We advance it as an alternative suggestion. The advantage of this way of looking at it is that it is highly unlikely that decisions by Department II will turn out just so that equilibrium is restored within the same period as Marx's numerical examples seem to show. It does not imply that Department II drives the system, any more than the original Marx example says that Department I drives the system. It is the gap in profit rates between Departments that initiates the disequilibrium and it is in the attempt to equalize the rate of profits across Departments that the system moves forward.

The formalization of this process is not attempted here but will be developed in another context. For the time being let us put forward another way of recasting equation (16) to bring it into line with Bortkiewicz's original formulation. We recall that in Bortkiewicz's case we wrote the identity for total value as

$$p_1 C + p_2 V + p_3 S = C + V + S = Y_1 + Y_2 + Y_3 = Y \qquad (11)$$

As explained above in the example of expanded reproduction Marx put forward p_3 and Y_3 are zero. Surplus value must either take the forms of C or V. A proportion β of S will take the form of C depending pn the accumulation decisions in Department I and Department II. The remainder will be spent on wage goods partly as addition to V but partly as capitalists consumption, which in the end will appear as no different from workers expenditure. Thus instead of (16) we get

$$p_1(C + \beta S) + p_2(V + (1-\beta)S) = C + V + S = Y_1 + Y_2 = Y \qquad (18)$$

This gets instead of the system (17) a system in which only the last equation is changed to

$$367\, p_1 + 116\, p_2 + (p_1 \beta + p_2(1-\beta))\ 116 = 483$$

96

We have four unknowns now p_1, p_2, ρ and β, the proportion accumulated which will solve for the other three unknowns. As we emphasized above, this way of presenting the problem makes the choice of β arbitrary and does not link it with the process of capitalist production i.e. prices and the rate of profit. Many economic models assume $\beta = 1$ (capitalists do not consume) or β related to the propensity to save.[3] In fact, β *is not given from outside but is itself determined by* p_1, p_2, ρ *in a complicated but as yet never satisfactorily specified manner.* We could go on to assume β given arbitrarily and solve for the prices and rate of profit but that would be misleading.

In his book Morishima has generalised the mathematical representation of Marx's example[4] He also assumes a common propensity to save α but includes in αS the spending on C as well as on V. Thus the division of αS_1, say, into C_1 and V_1 is determined by g_1. The process by which α is determined is not investigated by Morishima but he does allow that, unlike in Marx's model, capitalists can invest in either Department given that the same equilibrium rate of profit prevails in both Departments. He does not therefore concern himself with Rosa Luxemburg's problem of the process by which such equilibrium is established.

Morishima's mathematical presentation allows him to say that the system of expanded reproduction will not be stable but explosive. It will be explosive with oscillations if g_2 is greater than g_1 - the organic composition of capital in Department II exceeds that in Department I. It will be explosive without oscillation otherwise. Thus the dilemma which troubled Marx and Rosa Luxemburg - the steady expansion of capitalism in the example given by Marx and the uneven development observed in 19th century capitalism-can be seen as being a consequence of the rigid assumption made about the proportion of surplus value invested by Department I, the lack of mobility of capital between the two Departments and the passive behaviour of capitalists in Department II.

While Morishima's model generates cycles and even cycles of increasing severity, it seems to depend on a mathematical condition, i.e. a constant, exogenously given value of α. Cycles have not been explosive in the history of capitalism (though many Marxists would say that this is because two world wars have interrupted the course of cycles). The task is therefore to generate cycles which can be of increasing severity but in which the system responds to its historical experience and finds ways of moderating this severity. Morishima also poses the problem in value terms entirely and does not pose the question of cycles in prices and profits. Yet, while the process of uneven development is a mathematical result, it is also - and much more importantly - a historical process. Exports of capital, tariffs, devaluations, customs unions, imperialist expansion, wasteful expenditure - all these events occur as part of the capitalist system's attempt to overcome the problems of uneven development. Now that the mathematical puzzles have been solved and Marx's arithmetical example tidied up (by Morishima, for example) attempts should be made to pose the problem as one of historical development. The previous pages represent a preliminary effort to do so.

THE FALLING RATE OF PROFIT

The long standing neglect of Marx in traditional economic theory (and in the wider intellectual context) has been based on two main criticisms. Firstly, following Bohm-Bawerk, Wicksteed and others, it is claimed that the labour theory of value is erroneous and unnecessary as an explanation of relative prices. Marx's failure 'to prove' that prices are proportional to labour content in Vol. III, as against his assertion of such proportionality in Vol. I, is thought to have settled the matter. The labour theory of value is assigned then to the status of theories which have been superseded by better ones - we could call this 'the labour theory as Flat Earth view'. This view also implies that empirically it is obvious that prices are not proportional to labour content anyway - that the Earth is round. Thus both logically and empirically the labour theory of value according to this view is superseded and its continuing defence is dogmatic.

This argument, in our view, has missed the main purpose of labour theory of value in Marx. Once his arithmetical errors have been corrected (as by Bortkiewicz) prices are derivable from (though not proportional to) value categories. We should add, however, that both logically and empirically the translation of values into prices (and vice versa) while important in order to bring out the social dynamics is a much more complex task than either critics or defenders of Marx have ever previously allowed for.

The second criticism is that Marx's prophecies have been contradicted by the course of capitalist society. The working class is not immiserised either relatively or absolutely: socialist revolutions have failed to occur in mature capitalist countries; full employment rather than the reserve army of unemployed is the order of the day and the rate of profit has not fallen as Marx predicted it would.[1]

It would be fruitless to deny that 20th century capitalism, especially post-1945 post-Keynesian capitalism, contradicts many of the gloomy prophecies. Many defenders of Marx have tried to redefine and rationalise the predictions in a way that they come out to be valid or at least not contradicted. Thus the less developed third world is seen to be the reserve army of unemployed; their people are the increasingly immiserised proletariat. There were even attempts, happily forgotton now, to prove that the increasing productivity of the modern worker meant increasing relative rate of exploitation and hence increasing misery in psychological terms. We do not wish to take up such a last ditch defence position. We shall concern ourselves with the question of testing Marx's predictions especially the prediction about the falling rate of profit.

In the following pages we look at Marx's statement of the problem and at least one detailed attempt (by Gillman) to test the prediction. We examine the problem of testing the prediction particularly in the light of our discussions about the value-price transformation problem. Once again, it emerges that Marx's predictions are testable (i.e. they are falsifiable) but that the test is complex and may be very difficult to carry out. Such tests as have been rigorously performed or casually carried out up to now make crucial assumptions about value-price proportionality which render them invalid. Marx's discussion of the law of the falling rate of profit or the law of the tendency of the rate of profit to fall is stated in terms of a one good model. The relevant rate of profit here is what we have called the value rate of profit. Readers will recall that in his erroneous solution of the Transformation problem, Marx required each industry to earn an average (value) rate of profit equal to $\bar{p}$ where $\bar{p} = S/C + V$. In Part III of *Capital* Vol. III, Marx discussed the conditions for the law to hold.

To begin with, *assuming a given wage and a given length of working day*, Marx is able to express variable capital as an index number of labourers (note the assumptions carefully). Now if a given number of workers is presented with an increasing *quantity* of material means of production, this is also likely to mean a growing *value* (not necessarily

100

equiproportionate) of constant capital accompanying the given amount of value of variable capital. Now a constant rate of surplus value under these assumptions tautologically indicates a falling rate of profit since, as we have seen before,

$$\bar{p} = r(1 - \frac{C}{C + V}) = r(1 - g)$$

The question of the general validity of any law therefore does not depend on the formula above but in the assumptions made about the behaviour of the components r, C and V.

We have here two measures being employed simultaneously. Firstly is the ratio of labourers (working a given number of hours at a given wage) to the quantity of raw materials and the quantity of machinery and fixed capital. This is the physical input ratio (which raises many complex problems of measuring the *quantity* of machines independent of the profit and price information). Then we have the total value of constant capital and variable capital and the corresponding expression of the organic composition of capital. Similarly the output of all this activity can be measured in physical units ("the real mass of use-values") or in value terms. By assuming a given rate of surplus value, we are saying that surplus value is the same amount as variable capital but we are not saying anything about the ratio of physical units of output per worker or per hour worked. Thus requires further information about productivity etc.

There is a third measure which is directly observable in terms of prices. These are the recorded figures of wages, costs, profits, prices etc. In testing the Marxian prediction, we have to use data on money value of profits (strictly all non-wage income) and compare it with an appropriate measure of constant and variable capital in price terms. We have already seen that even in simple reproduction with given constant magnitudes of r and g_i, prices are not proportional to values. With extended reproduction, changing magnitudes of g_i (and also r) as well as increasing physical productivity and decreasing length of working day the price-value translation is even more difficult. Any casual empiricism about the rate of profit derived from the published national income and wealth statistics is not much help here.

Now during the process of growth, the physical productivity of labour power in both the Departments goes up; hence the same value amounts represent progressively higher physical quantities of machines and wage goods. Growth of productivity in wage goods industry can reduce the value of labour power since it will take less time to reproduce itself; the effect of such productivity on wages is not easy to predict since it will depend on the strength of the working class and the historical course of the class struggle. Only in a mechanical, ahistorical model of Marxian economic theory does the real wage rate always equal the subsistence level and hence the value of labour power. Such a model allows no scope for changing class relations and by divorcing the model from social relations reduces a Marxian model to a Ricardian model of labour theory of value.

Changing the ratio of value to physical units would slow down the tendency of the rate of profit to fall since the physical ratios can go up much faster than value ratios. A change in the ratio can occur not only due to growing productivity but also as a result of foreign trade. If we treat all developed capitalist countries as a system then such trade must be with the non-capitalist and pre-capitalist countries. This point has already been mentioned in connection with Rosa Luxemburg's solution of the problem of extended reproduction and will not therefore be further elaborated here. We need to add however that if such trade is reinforced by the unequal status involved in a colonial relationship, the price-value ratio may also be favourable to the developed metropolitan country in addition to the lowering of value due to trade.

The law relates to the (value) rate of profit and does not make predictions about the amount of total surplus value, or the amount of money profits, though in general the amount of profit (the mass of profits) may go up since as the total amount of capital goes up, a tendency for surplus value (or surplus) to rise is not necessarily in contradiction with the falling rate of profit. Nor is there any clear-cut prediction here about the share of profits or wages in income. Since the problem has never been analytically formulated fully in a way that will allow for all the dynamic elements mentioned on the previous page, the prediction in Marx's theory regarding the share of

102

profits is ambiguous. Marxist economists in recent years have tried
to develop models of contemporary capitalism dealing with each of
these two aspects - rising amount of surplus and rising share of wages
in income - but it must be said that these models stand in no clear
relation to the law of the falling rate of profit.

The notion of constant capital is taken in the sense of the amount
used up during the production period. This is a flow concept corresponding to physical depreciation plus user cost in the Keynesian
sense. This however adds the additional complication that the rate
of use of capital (the period of turnover) may also change due to
technology and also as a corrective response to the falling rate of
profit on the part of the capitalists. This makes the measurement of
the rate of profit all the harder because depreciation is also
influenced by accounting conventions, tax laws and fiscal policies
designed especially to boost investment.

Mention must be made at this stage of the possible counteracting
forces noted by Marx. We have already discussed the possible cheapening of elements of capital and foreign trade. There is also the
additional possibility of increasing the rate of surplus value. This
can be done absolutely by increasing the length of the working day
though this does not imply that at any point of time the country with
a longer working day has the higher rate of surplus value. Alternatively, the intensity of work and the productivity of the worker may
increase the rate of exploitation relatively. Growth of concentration
of capital and monopolistic tendencies have also been mentioned but,
given the aggregate notion of the rate of profit, it is difficult to
relate these factors analytically to the general proposition.

It is well known that a law of falling rate of profit is a
recurring theme in classical political economy. Adam Smith, Ricardo
and John Stuart Mill each enunciated such a law.[2] The stationary
state corresponding to the zero rate of profit also meant different
things to these economists. John Stuart Mill contemplated the
stationary state with pleasurable anticipation. In Marx, the role of
the falling rate of profit is different. The tendency of the rate of
profit to fall illustrated   the second contradiction of capitalism.
The first contradiction is the emergence of free labour and the class

monopoly of means of production. The second contradicition is the growing disparity between the productive capacity of the system - the productive potential and the actual output as dictated by the profit motive. Reproduction in a capitalist system for Marx is not the production of use values - not production for the sake of eventual consumption. Production is the production of capital in such a way that expansion of capital occurs - production for profit and for increased accumulation. The falling rate of profit comes about because of the tendency of the system to concentrate on surplus value and to replace variable capital by constant capital. The capacity of the productive system to produce use values is continually increasing but the falling rate of profit prevents it from fully realising this potential capacity. It is in order to illustrate this contradiction that the tendency of falling rate of profit is crucial to Marxian economic theory.[3]

GILLMAN'S TEST OF THE FALLING RATE OF PROFIT [1]

Joseph Gillman in his book *The Falling Rate of Profit* has
subjected the law to a series of tests using US data for the period
1849-1952. As far as I know, no attempt has been made to bring these
calculations up to date. Gillman in using published data identifies
the value categories directly with the price categories. Thus
variable capital is measured in his calculations by the wage bill for
production workers; constant capital by the cost of materials (and
where available) the amount set aside as depreciation, depletion and
amortization. He has carried out these calculations for all manufacturing industries. We summarise all his calculations in Table V at the
end of the Chapter. They are as follows:

(1) Using Census of Manufacturing data decennially for 1849-1899,
quinquennially for 1899-1919 and bienially for 1919-1939. Since
census data did not publish depreciation the cost of materials was
taken to measure constant capital (C) and wages of production workers
to measure variable capital (V). Surplus value was measured as value
of product minus ($C + V$), or equivalently as value added less V.[2] As
we can see in columns 1a - 1c, the organic composition of capital
(defined as C/V) goes up from 2.3 in 1849 to 3.8 in 1919 but remains
more or less constant around a lower figure of 3.5 thereafter. The
rate of surplus value goes up from 1849-1919 and after a drop in 1921
goes up until 1929 but is cyclical with a slight downward trend afterwards. The rate of profit in column 1c shows no trend that can be
discerned but more a tendency to cyclical fluctuations. These calculations therefore show that up to 1919 the rise in C/V was compensated by

a rise in r to yield no trend in p. After 1919, the cycles in p are pronounced but still there is no downward trend; if anything the trend is upward.

(2) Combining the biennial census data with annual data from the Bureau of Internal Revenue, Gillman produces an annual series on $\bar{p}$ for 1919-1939, after some adjustments (e.g. splicing) have been made. These figures include depreciation as published by the Bureau of Internal Revenue. These data are in columns 2a - 2c. Here again there is no clear upward or downward trend in any of the three ratios. There is some case for arguing in favour of an upward trend in r and $\bar{p}$ for 1919-1939 and a downward trend or constancy afterwards. In general, $\bar{p}$ shows no downward trend by this calculation.

(3) Since the ratio of depreciation (and user cost) to stock of capital could be varying, Gillman computed the rate of profit on stock of capital. The stock of fixed capital was measured as "the values of plant and equipment taken at their reproduction costs at current prices net of depreciation." [3] These differ from book values since these are often in historical value. Using these figures, there is a decline in the rate of profit for 1880-1919 but no trend from 1919-1952. These are listed in columns 3a - 3c. Including the stock of fixed capital and circulating capital - inventories - similar results are obtained as in columns 3a - 3c. These do not add anything of substance.

(4) Gillman does a further calculation by deducting from his measure of surplus value a measure of unproductive expenditure. These would comprise selling costs, employment of non-production workers etc. This item is measured as the gap between surplus value and net profits plus rent and interest paid. He calculates $p_1 = S - u/C$ on a stock measure of C and $p_2 = S - u/C + V + u$ as a flow measure on the argument that being costs of realising surplus value, u should be added to total capital used up in producing surplus value. $\bar{p}_1$ figures for 1919, 1929 and 1939 are 15.4%, 12.5% and 11.1% respectively. $\bar{p}_2$ figures for the same three years are 12.0%, 9.6% and 8.2%. If government activity is regarded as an alternative measure of unproductive expenditure, then we can also net out total tax collections from profits. For 1929, 1939 and 1949, Gillman deducts Federal and State corporation income

and excess profits taxes from surplus value and gets a measure of rate of profit for these years as 24.2%, 21.7% and 17.0% respectively. Data for $\bar{p}_1$ and $\bar{p}_2$ are given in columns 4a - 4b.

On balance, one can say that the rate of profit as measured by Gillman in flow terms does not decline. When adjustments are made on a stock basis there is some tendency for a decline in the 1880 - 1919 period. If we accept unproductive expenditure as a deduction from surplus value then the post-1919 period also shows a decline. It must be said however that these tests are not decisive either way. The use of national income statistics and census data involves many measurement problems which complicate testing of hypotheses even in mainstream economic theory. These data involve inaccuracies, measurement errors and index number problems. These are not reflections on the quality of Gillman's workmanship but complications of testing theories against inadequate real world data. Imperfect as it may be, it was a pioneering effort at empirical work in Marxian economics which unfortunately has not been followed up for other countries or other periods.[4]

The problem is also with the Marx's theoretical formulation of the law as we have repeatedly emphasised. Not only is the law not stated by Marx in terms of the money rate of profit, but even on the value basis there are unspecified assumptions regarding increasing productivity, rate of turnover, changing length of working day etc. The law needs to be reformulated in as far as it is possible allowing for such complications. Then the problem of transformation needs to be tackled. Only then can we use published data, imperfect as they will surely be, to verify the law.

Gillman's treatment of unproductive expenditure may appear arbitrary, a way of rationalizing the data in favour of Marx. We shall go into this question of unproductive expenditure when we consider recent developments in Marxian economic theory. At the present, Gillman's treatment points to the fact that *even as formulated by Marx, the law of the falling rate of profit does not allow for problems of realizing surplus valu* . This is because it is cast in a one-good framework using only value categories. Since prices do not systematically enter the law, the problem of realization of surplus value has no obvious place. The situation is similar to Marx's model of extended

reproduction which assumed away crises in constructing the arithmetic
examples. Once again the circuit of money capital is ignored in Marx
formulation whereas in the real world these monetary and financial
factors are interwoven into the economic fabric with other factors.
treating selling costs as unproductive expenditure to be netted out
of surplus value, Gillman is taking the view that these are costs of
realization and a deduction from the amount available for accumulatio
in the future. A similar argument can be made about the government
sector since by keeping up effective demand, but without generating
material output, government expenditure ceases the realization proble

The law of the tendency of the rate of the profit to fall is, in
conclusion, neither well specified nor unambiguously seen to be prove
or disproved. The difficulty is that both the defenders and detracto
of Marx have stayed within the terms defined by Marx. Even when mode
mathematical tools have been applied in this respect, they have only
tidied up certain inconsistencies and solved old puzzles. The theory
has not been further developed in the spirit in which Marx initiated
it using his tools. Rosa Luxemburg was of course the singular excep-
tion. She asked original critical questions and was not satisfied
with accepting the problem as stated and solved by Marx. Mainstream
economics has not gone on to develop Marx's model in his terms becaus
it has clearly other tools and other concerns. The task of developing
Marx's model has fallen to Marxist economists. We shall see below how
they have met the challenge. It is clear that there exists no agreed
body of analytical models developing further from Marx's theory which
either enrich Marx's model or bring it into relation with new developments in capitalism. This is not to say that many have not worked in
this area. However, when we look at their contributions we find that
for various reasons - some of which have been political or ideologica]
there is no substantial body of ongoing work in the Marxian paradigm
which can be taken with any seriousness.

TABLE V

Gillman's calculations of the rate of profit

	1a	1b	1c	2a	2b	2c	3a	3b	3c	4a	4b
	g	r(%)	p	g	r(%)		g	r	p	$\bar{p}_1$	$\bar{p}_2$
1849	2.3	96	29								
1859	2.7	125	34								
1869	3.2	125	30								
1879	3.6	108	24				0.8	102	122		
1889₁	2.7	123	33				1.1	114	102		
1899₂	3.2	144	35				1.7	132	79		
1899²	3.4	145	33								
1904	3.4	147	34								
1909₃	3.7	155	33								
1914³	3.7	148	32				2.3	137	61		
1919	3.8	147	31	3.9	135	27.6	3.2	125	40	15.4	12.0
1920				3.4	111	25.2	3.1			9.2	8.0
1921	3.3	132	31	3.5	116	26.0	4.1	103	25	2.0	2.1
1922				3.5	124	27.2	3.5			10.6	9.8
1923	3.3	142	33	3.5	128	28.6	3.0	121	41	12.2	9.8
1924				3.6	131	28.9	3.2			10.2	8.3
1925	3.5	157	35	3.7	142	30.3	3.1	136	44	11.4	8.8
1926				3.6	140	30.4	3.0			11.8	9.4
1927	3.4	161	37	3.6	144	31.6	3.1	139	45	10.0	8.0
1928				3.7	159	34.1	3.2			11.9	9.3
1929	3.4	181	41	3.6	164	35.4	3.1	159	51	12.5	9.6
1930				3.6	161	35.0	3.7			5.7	4.9
1931	3.2	178	43	3.5	154	34.4	4.4	147	33	1.3	1.2
1932				3.6	145	31.5	5.6			-	-
1933	3.4	184	42	3.7	154	32.9	4.9	150	31	3.4	3.8
1934				3.6	137	29.6	4.0			5.8	5.6
1935	3.6	154	33	3.8	136	28.2	3.4	130	38	8.9	7.2
1936				4.0	150	30.2	3.0			11.9	8.6
1937	3.5	149	33	3.7	134	28.6	2.7	130	48	11.0	7.9
1938				3.9	149	30.6	3.5			5.9	4.7
1939	3.5	172	38	3.7	149	32.0	3.0	151	50	11.1	8.2
1940							2.8				
1941							2.2				
1942							1.8				
1943							1.5				
1944							1.5				
1945							1.9				
1946							2.3				
1947							2.4	129	54		
1948							2.5				
1949							2.8	129	46		
1950							2.7	141	53		
1951							2.6	133	52		
1952							2.6	132	51		

Notes:

Gillman's measure of the organic composition of capital (g) is C/V rather than $C/C + V$ as we have defined it.

(1) Includes factories and land and neighbourhood industries up to 1899 in cols. 1a - 1c.

(2) Excludes the items mentioned in (1) above from now on.

(3) Includes establishments having products valued at $500 or more as hitherto. Subsequent to 1914, only such establishments were included in the census as had products valued at $5000 or more. The effect, as in the preceding case, was to lift the organic composition of capital somewhat.

The first four entries in Tables 3a - 3c are for 1880, 1890, 1900 and 1912 rather than 1879, 1889, 1899 and 1914.

CONTEMPORARY RELEVANCE OF MARXIAN ECONOMIC THEORY

In discussing the relevance of Marxian economic theory to contemporary problems, we touch upon a topic where there are more areas of unfinished research than of agreed results. For about forty years after Marx there was in Germany and Russia a living Marxist tradition. In these years, many who were active socialists as well as keen debaters examined their contemporary reality in the light of Marxian theory. They took up the challenge of adapting Marx, of adding to his analysis and of deriving practical lessons from it. These were years of bitter sectarian debate often carried out under a constant threat of political persecution when major decisions had to be made by these parties. From 1883, when Marx died, up to about 1928 before the end of the debate in the Soviet Union, there continued to pour out many Marxian writings. Many who were neither Marxists nor socialists entered the debate from academic curiosity - Bortkiewicz being a prime example. In these forty years the task was begun, though not satisfactorily concluded, of providing a theory of economic crises, an area in which Marx had made many suggestions but provided no complete theory. The extension of Marxian theory to cover agrarian change and the problem of backward countries was tackled by Kautsky and Lenin among others. After 1917 the task of the optimal strategy for growth was debated in Russia. In these years, Marxian economics was developed by, among others, Lenin, Rosa Luxemburg, Kautsky, Bernstein, Danielson, Vorontsov, Tugan Baranowsky, Bukharin, Preobrazhensky, Trotsky, Grossman, Bulgakov, Struve, Hilferding and Bortkiewicz.[1]

The suppression of political debate in the Soviet Union and the defeat of the socialist and communist parties which coincided with the rise of Hitler in Germany ended the long tradition of Marxian theoretical debate in the two countries where it had been most alive. In the English speaking countries, Marxism had never been a very powerful intellectual force. Intellectually, economic theory was now entirely in the Jevons-Walras tradition. Even when a theoretical revolution occurred in economics the effect was to confirm the exiled status of Marxian economics. The Keynesian revolution took place without any reference to Marx though many young economists in the 1930's sought to draw parallels between Marxian and Keynesian economics, to translate one in terms of the other, to claim that Keynes vindicated Marx and gave the best rationale for socialism.[2]

The revival of interest in Marxian economic theory in the post-war period was slow. The years of the cold war with McCarthyism in the US and Stalinist orthodoxy in the USSR diverted such discussion as there was into sterile channels. The mechanical and apocalyptic aspects of Marx were emphasised; mistakes in his analysis were not admitted at all or covered by apologia. In the late 1950's the emergence of the *New Left* in Europe and more recently the student movement in North America and Europe, the liberation movement in many colonial territories, the Chinese and the Cuban Revolutions have all contributed to bring about the resurgence of interest in Marxian economics.

Much effort is spent by each new generation in learning the essentials of Marx's theory and about old debates and puzzles. The central problem however is whether Marxian economic theory is relevant for an analysis of contemporary capitalism. Many changes have occurred during the development of capitalism in the last hundred years since Marx wrote. Capitalism in the post-1945 years can boast of full employment, high and rising standards of living and a comparatively peaceful period of development. In the 1950's and 1960's it was thought by many that the desire for a higher standard of living, especially for the new consumers' durables, had blunted the militant edge of the working class. Even the very notion of a class society is questioned by many. Economic activity seemed to be running free of crises and with a high degree of consensus about aims of economic policy. The Keynesian revolution had apparently provided a panacea for the ills of capitalism that Marx had analysed.

In the last five years with the problems of inflation and of unstable international monetary movements, many economists and statesmen have come to pronounce the death of Keynes. In dealing with inflation, many western policy makers have begun to talk in terms of the political economy of the problem. Workers and their militant attitudes expressed either through official Trade Union channels or unofficially are seen to be a new problem. Many have sought to pose the problems in terms of political power of the different participants - workers, employers and the governments.[3]

Despite this temporary eclipse in his reputation, the challenge of Keynes to Marx remains. The very success of post-Keynesian capitalism has shifted the basis of Marxian critique of capitalism. Before capitalism was criticised for failing to realise its full productive potential, thriving on a perpetual reserve army of unemployed, making glaring the contradiction between the forces of production and relations of production. By contrast, socialism as embodied in the USSR was seen to guarantee full employment and rapid industrialisation. Now the criticism is on the wastefulness of capitalism. Post-Keynesian prosperity is maintained, it is said, on the basis of wasteful expenditure on armaments and luxury goods. This expenditure guarantees a high rate of profit in the private economy by easing the realization problem since income is created in this 'third' sector of armaments without creating marketable output. There is however no permanent solution to the problems of capitalism in such wastefulness; sooner or later the contradictions will re-emerge with greater forcefulness and engulf the system.

These criticisms can be discussed here briefly in the context of the works of Baran and Sweezy and of Mattick. We shall inspect the analytical models used by these authors and examine them in the light of the Marxian models. There are many other areas covered by them which we shall ignore. Thus we shall not try to examine the existing state of wealth and income distribution to advance evidence on the class structure of modern capitalist societies. We do not enter here into the question of the trend of concentration of economic power in the hands of large corporations. It is not the purpose here to develop a critique of capitalist societies or of any one country such as USA.

These tasks are important but outside the scope of this short work.

Baran and Sweezy in the *Monopoly Capital* do not use the value system at all. They argue for the abandonment of the law of the falling Rate of Profit and its replacement by the Law of Rising Surplus. They abandon the distinction between the value system and the price system. All their analysis is in terms of price relationships substantiated by citing statistics couched in terms of exchange relationship - wages, profits, costs etc. They argue that Marx's scheme was valid for a world where competition prevailed among the firms. In the current stage of monopoly capitalism, the value scheme and especially the surplus value notion is no longer appropriate. They emphasise the need for a new theory. This concerns itself with "the generation and absorption of the surplus under conditions of monopoly capitalism." (*Monopoly Capital*, p.8).[4]

"Economic surplus" is defined by Baran and Sweezy as "the difference between what a society produces and the costs of producing it. The size of the surplus is an index of productivity and wealth, of how much freedom a society has to accomplish whatever goals it may set for itself. The composition of the surplus shows how it uses that freedom; how much it invests in expanding its productive capacity, how much it consumes in various forms and how much it wastes and in what ways." (pp. 9-10).

On the basis of an analysis of US Income and Expenditure Data for 1929 - 1963 by Joseph Phillips, Baran and Sweezy enunciate two tendencies. A tendency for the share of surplus in GNP to rise and a tendency for property income (which they identify with Marxian surplus value) as a share of surplus to fall. The growing size of surplus and its growing share illustrates for Baran and Sweezy the irrationally utilised portion of a society's income. Thus potentially this growing surplus could be utilised for egalitarian purposes but it is not so utilised. The analysis and measurement of surplus plays a role as a critical tool in pointing out the irrationality and wastefulness of capitalism.

"Monopoly capitalism is a system made up of giant corporations" according to Baran and Sweezy (p. 52). Monopolies tend to set prices by mutually collusive agreements whether tacit or open. The pressure of competition between these corporations makes itself felt as a pressure to reduce costs by introducing new technological innovations. This then leads to a tendency for monopoly profits to rise. "The whole motivation of cost reduction is to increase profits, and the monopolistic structure of markets enables the corporations to appropriate the lion's share of the fruits of increasing productivity directly in the form of higher profits. This means that under monopoly capitalism declining costs imply continuously widening profit margins. And continuously widening profit margins in turn imply aggregate profits which rise not only absolutely but as a share of national product. If we provisionally equate aggregate profits with society's economic surplus, we can formulate as a law of monopoly capitalism that the surplus tends to rise both absolutely and relatively as the system develops." (pp. 71-72).

But while monopoly capitalism generates rising surplus, it does not provide channels either in investment or capitalists' consumption to absorb the surplus. Baran and Sweezy then list the expenditure on advertising, the growing expenditure of civilian government and the growth of armaments as the wasteful channels which absorb the surplus and keep the system growing and avoiding stagnation. Selling costs incurred in advertising are clearly the costs of realisation of surplus value in the original Marxian framework. This was indeed how Gillman treated selling costs in testing the law of falling rate of profit as we saw above. The expenditure of governments for civilian and defence purposes when financed out of a net addition to National Debt is regarded by Baran and Sweezy as a Keynesian measure to ensure a high level of demand which keeps up prices by easing the realisation problem.

There are many similarities between Rosa Luxemburg's analysis of the Third Department and Baran and Sweezy's analysis of monopoly capitalism. They, however, abandon completely the value framework and either identify surplus value with national income categories (e.g. profits and interest and rent) or avoid the use of this concept. The unsolved problems in Marxian value analysis are thus left unsolved. Even the introduction of monopoly element in the analysis does not examine, for example, how the relationship between the organic composition of capital (or its physical counterpart) and the rate of surplus

value is different under monopoly capital. Their analysis draws on
Neoclassical economic theory in the tradition of Marshall as outlined
by Joan Robinson in her *Economics of Imperfect Competition* and E.H.
Chamberlin in *The Theory of Monopolistic Competition*. The tools
employed by these authors are those of demand curves and cost curves
without any reference to the theory of surplus value.

It may be that in common with many other economists, for example
Morishima whose work we outlined above, Baran and Sweezy wanted to
urge the dropping of the value scheme altogether. But then they do
not replace the value scheme by a new theory in a Marxian framework.
Their analysis of the behaviour of corporations follows very closely
John Kenneth Galbraith's theories of the New Industrial State. Their
statistical investigations of the surplus have been anticipated in
traditional macro-economics by the measure known as the full employment
surplus or the Okun gap.[5] This is the gap between the potential level
of GNP at full employment level and the actual level at any time. It
is used for operational purposes of macroeconomic stabilisation. The
label Baran and Sweezy attach to this concept is critical but its
function can be easily operational. Baran and Sweezy's analysis is
then a combination of Neoclassical microeconomics, without the assumption
of perfect competition, and orthodox macroeconomics. The question
whether Marxian economic theory is relevant to contemporary capitalism
can be easily answered in the negative after reading *Monopoly Capital*.[6]

Paul Mattick in his *Marx and Keynes* has taken up the challenge of
evaluating Keynes' theory in the light of Marxian theory. His task is
not to extend or amend Marx's model but take account of any new developments. He is more concerned with asserting that Marx anticipated many
of Keynes' findings. What is good and insightful in Keynes is already
in Marx; Keynes' solution for the problems of capitalism can only be
a temporary solution - this is the central thesis of Mattick's book[7].

Much of Mattick's book is an exposition of Keynes' theory and of
Marx's theory. In evaluating Keynes' theory, Mattick says "Marx
anticipated Keynes' criticism of the Neoclassical theory through his
own criticism of classicial theory; and both men recognized the capitalist dilemma in a declining rate of capital formation." (p.21). "Marx's
capital analysis" Mattick says "has proved to have great predictive

power. The actual course of capital accumulation followed its general outline of development. Indeed, the course of capital development as predicted by Marx has never been denied; other explanations merely state the reason for this trend differently. Keynes offered one of these explanations." (p.109).

Mattick accounts for the continued prosperity of capitalism by emphasising the role of the two World Wars in destroying accumulated capital stock and thus restoring profitability. In the post 1945 years he gives a similar role to armaments. "Full use of productive resources, where and when it came about, was accomplished by extending government-induced 'non-profitable' production. Part of this increase resulted from public welfare and foreign-aid measures; most of it was generated by military expenditures.... It was by way of inflation, debt-accumulation, government-induced production, war-preparation and actual warfare that the dominant capitalist nations reached an approximation of full employment." (pp.122 - 123). In earlier years, business cycles performed the task of destroying accumulated capital. But according to Mattick, at the turn of the century, a point was reached whereby cycles were no longer sufficient. "The business cycle as an instrument of accumulation had apparently come to an end; or, rather, the business cycle became a 'cycle' of world wars." (p.135).

While Marx did not foresee many of these events, Mattick says, they are perfectly consistent with his theory. Indeed the rise of Keynesianism is a socio-economic development predicted by Marx's theory, according to Mattick. (p.130). What is more, state intervention to achieve full employment is not even a new socio-economic development which need be *predicted* by Marx. It is a part of Marx's theory anyway. "Marx's theory does not deny the fact that full-employment can and may be created either by government-induced investments or by an increase in the propensity to consume." (p. 131). For Mattick thus the Keynesian challenge is no challenge; it is all in Marx and not a word of it needs revising, adapting or correcting.

In essence then Mattick's response to Keynesian theory is to assert the continued validity of Marx's analysis. He does not advance the analytical problem by solving any of the puzzles pointed out by Rosa Luxemburg or evident on reading *Capital*. His main point is that

117

governments cannot create new demand; they only redistribute the surplus value which is already there. He does not however demonstrate this in a value theoretic model using, say, a three Department scheme. He also mentions the possibility of inflation arising from deficit financing, but once again no analysis is carried out in either value or price framework.

What can one say about *Marx and Keynes*? The need to assert Marx's eternal validity and the ultimate apocalypse of capitalism is quite strong among Marxian economists, but much more than that needs to be done. While a full treatment is out of the question here, several points are worth emphasis.

The interpretation of Keynes is in itself a controversial matter to this day. The conventional textbook treatment is more Hicksian than Keynesian, as has been pointed out by Leijonhufvud.[8] The irrationality of the process which generates businessmen's expectations and the consequent volatility of the Investment Schedule have been pointed out again by Shackle.[9] In this sense, the investment decision is crucial to Marx and Keynes in their analysis of capitalist development. Marx had two hypotheses about investment - an inherent drive to accumulate as a result of competitive pressures and accumulation in order to maintain the rate of profit but in his arithmetical example in Vol. II he assumed an arbitrary $\frac{1}{2}$ proportion being accumulated from surplus value of Department I. In order to maintain the rate of profit however the capitalist need not accumulate. He may export capital, spend surplus value on consumption or waste it on other unproductive expenditure. Of these factors, only the export of capital was given prominence by Marx. The disposal of surplus value to maintain the rate of profit and in consequence the reduction in rate of accumulation has to be formalised in a value theoretic model. In this case, the springs for accumulation must be sought in exchange relationship and their consequences in the value relationship.

A more important common element is that both Marx and Keynes are monetary economists. For Marx, the crucial difference was between money as a hoard or as a medium of exchange and money as money capital. Only when money was advanced in the productive process did it function for Marx as money capital. Unfortunately this part of Marx's theory has been left undeveloped. The development of the money circuit of capital and its integration with the commodity circuit is an important area for research in Marxian economics. Keynes' monetary theory in this respect is similar but it has no links with the commodity circuit since this aspect is left unspecified by him.

In this context, it is important to bring out the role of the interest rate. Since Marx regarded the interest income as a portion of surplus value, Marxists have tended to ignore interest rate movements. Many Neoclassical economists on the other hand have tried to prove that a pure rate of interest exists in all economies (including a capitalist economy) independent of the productive process and hence of exploitation. Thus, the Wicksellian example of maturing wine creating surplus value by the mere passage of time has been recently cited by Weiszacker in his criticism of Morishima.[10] Samuelson also points out in referring to Adam Smith's primitive economy that "Rude economies are not low or zero interest economies; they tend to be high interest states in which short term methods are used precisely because of the very 'scarcity of time'....."[11] A distinction should be made however between the concept of the pure rate of interest as an intertemporal accounting device and interest as forming the income of a rentier class. One can analyse rude economies and study their techniques. In doing so, we may discover that a high shadow rate of interest exists in such economies. A socialist planner may choose the optimum rate of saving on the basis of such an accounting concept. *In neither situation need there be a class receiving interest incomes.* To Keynes, this was the crucial property of interest rate in capitalist economies. It formed the income of the rentier class; the expectations and the behaviour as a consequence of those expectations kept the interest up 'by its own bootstraps.' If interest rates formed an obstacle to investment plans it was because of this aspect of distribution between investors and rentiers. Its validity as a pure concept is less important than its existence as income for the rentier class and these must be kept separate. Similar remarks can be made about the rate of profit.

A fundamental difference arises between Marx and Keynes and indeed Marx and all other economists in their analysis of the labour market

Keynes emphasised that the labour market must be treated separately
from the money market and the commodity markets. The 'price' in the
labour market is determined by the money wage bargain and the institutional structure makes for the rigidity of the money wage. But as
Marx shows, the difference goes deeper. The price in the labour market
and the other main dimension - the length of the working day - are
determined by bargaining in the context of a class division. Labour
power can be bought like any other commodity under capitalism but the
exchange relationship here is based on a class relationship. The
'supply curve' of labour is not therefore analogous to that of, say,
bananas. Labourers can voluntarily withdraw labour, they can go on
strike, they can organize in trade unions, form political parties etc.
The wage bargain is the crucial dynamic element in Marx, expecially,
as we have already said above, the process whereby a gap develops between the wage rate and the value of labour power.

This has been emphasised in a recent book by Glyn and Sutcliffe.
In analysing the condition of British capitalism, Glyn and Sutcliffe[12]
point out that the declining profitability of British industries is
tied to a rising share of labour in national income, the stagnation
of the economy caused in its turn by the low level of investment due
to low profitability, and the increasing edge of international competition. By showing that the share of labour has risen in opposition
to the share of capital, they point out that, unlike in Neoclassical
models, high wages need not wait upon increasing accumulation and high
profits (see our discussion of Samuelson's 1971 article above). The
influence of workers' militancy, unionization and the overall political
context are also important. While they do not set up their model in
Marx's framework, they treat the wage bargain as a social and a political relation between the classes. They also emphasise the international contest within which such a study must be placed.

Glyn and Sutcliffe find that the share of profits in output has
been falling in the UK in the post-war period. There has been
especially an acceleration of this tendency since 1965. This decline
in the share of profits can be translated into a fall in the rate of
profit on capital. Their measure of the rate of profit on capital is
one which is widely accepted in current accounting practice. They do

not directly examine its relation to the Marxian rate of profit but qualitatively they set up a Marxian model by emphasising the role of the class struggle. They find that this tendency for the share of profit to fall is not confined to the UK alone but is true of most European capitalist countries. The decline was much less pronounced in the US, though even there in the late 1960's the situation worsened.

In Glyn and Sutcliffe's model, inflation (i.e. price raising) is a weapon used by the capitalists to cut into the gains made by workers during the wage bargain. Thus workers' gain, secured by militancy, tends to be eroded by inflation. There are however limits to the price increasing capacity of the capitalists of any one country. Faced with international competitiveness they either have to resist the wage rise demanded by the workers or suffer a fall in the profits by postponing the price rise or suffer a loss of markets. At the government level, exchange rate manipulation, i.e. devaluation, may offer a temporary breathing space and a gain in international comptitiveness, but there can be retaliation by other countries on this score.

Glyn and Sutcliffe have thus set up a model of wage determination incorporating class relations. Being a model of wage determination, it necessarily operates at the level of exchange relationships. This is as it should be. What Neoclassical economists call behavioural equations, whether on the part of the workers or of the capitalists, operate at the level of exchange relationship. Since the wage form dissolves the division of labour time between necessary and surplus labour, workers cannot react to changes in the rate of surplus value. It is only in Vol. III of *Capital* that Marx says that the rate of surplus value is equalised between industries by workers moving from one industry to another (III, pp. 153-154). This must now be regarded as a lapse on Marx's part in failing to maintain the distinction between value categories and price categories. Workers move from one industry to another (when they can) in search for higher wages. They strike and combine into trade unions for higher wages and shorter hours among a collection of economic and political demands. It is the task of the Marxian economist to try and analyse these phenomena in value terms. Is, for example, a rise in the share of wages in total output, consistent with a rising relative rate of surplus value (as a result of the capitalists' action to restore the rate of profit) as well as a rise in the share of surplus value, going to the workers? By translating an observable wage increase into the exchange *value* of labour power and a share of surplus value won by the workers from the capitalists, one can bring to bear the value apparatus to analyse such phenomena. This is especially useful for comparing the course of workers' struggle in different industries. We must begin by positing *unequal* rates of exploitation and a tendency towards equal rates of profit at the level of prices; equal exchange value of labour power in all industries and unequal organic composition of capitals in different industries. These elements can then combine into a model which will do justice to the full complexity of Marx's economics. If Marx took short cuts to make his arithmetical examples simpler, or if his work in its unfinished state (especially the two later volumes of *Capital*) contains errors, one must not dogmatically stick to them. We need not be in a hurry to reiterate every word he said. There is time enough to allow for the formulation and application of a richly complex model of values and to combine it with a model of prices and a model of physical production. This is the unfinished task of Marxian economic theory.

Chapter I

1 and 2. See the discussion in (23), especially the article by Lakatos. The whole question of 'science' and 'pseudo science' is complex and is not dealt with here at all. I have taken the position in this book that Marx's theory is a progressive research programme in Lakatos' terminology. Needless to say, this is a personal view which is as yet not fully developed.

Chapter II

1.   For the most recent and rigorous exposition of this view see (1).

2.   This is a very sketchy summary of the classical view. For further information see (4), (5), (13) and (35).

3.   The problem of an invariant measure of value is discussed in (44) and (13).

4.   For a bibliography see (42).

5.   The reference here is to (40). For an econometric application of this idea see (8).

6.   In Part VIII of *Capital*, Vol. I, Marx discusses the case of the USA and the low degree of exploitation there as a result of the availability of free land.

7.   This is a much debated issue. What I have given is a sketch of Marx's argument. In recent years, this view of the Enclosure movement has been challenged by historians. On the historical circumstances leading to the formation of the proletariat in England and the role of the Enclosure movement, see (10). A major omission in Marx's scheme is any mention of the formation of an agrarian labouring class. Marx more or less ignores the problem of agrarian class relations. It was left to Kautsky in (20) and Lenin in many of his pamphlets, but especially in (24), to take up the problem. The challenge posed by Chambers can be answered in terms of a Kautsky-Lenin agrarian class structure model, but this has never been satisfactorily done.

8.   It has been left to historians to bring out the particular circumstances underlying a general pattern. A particularly interesting example is Isaac Deutscher's discussion (12) of the changing class character of the Russian labour force after the Civil War and the importance it had in weakening the revolutionary tradition of the Russian proletariat. For the English case see (17).

* Numbers in parentheses refer to items in Bibliography

9. The ambiguities in the definition of the Bourgoisie has led to many problems for revolutionary governments. See, for example, Chapter 3 on "Class and Party" in (9).

10. This is no more than an outline of the standard Marxian position. Barrington Moore in (36) has illustrated the thesis with examples from many countries.

11. The three pamphlets by Marx on France (29), (30) and (31) illustra the full richness of a many class model in Marx's scheme.

12. See (16).

13. See (38). Both (16) and (38) are reprinted in (3).

Chapter III

1. See *Capital*, Vol. I, Chapter 1, Sections 1 and 4.

2. See the two pamphlets by Marx, *Wages, Price and Profit* (32) and *Wage, Labour and Capital* (33).

3. We ignore for the time being the merchant and the middleman. It i the capitalist as a producer we are interested in here.

4. See (44), Chapter VI.

Chapter V

1. *Capital*, Vol. II, Chapter 1.

2. For example see (27), Chapter 34.

3. *Capital*, Vol. I.

4. *Capital*, Vol. II.

5. For the input-output table, see (25). For Sraffa, see footnote 3 to Chapter II above.

Chapter VI

1. The models presented in this Chapter are derived from *Capital*, Vol. II. Marx uses the term 'extended reproduction'. I have used this interchangeably with the term 'expanded reproduction'.

Chapter VII

1. The word 'value' in this context means magnitude or amount. I ha tried as far as possible not to use the word value in this sense, but i is occasionally unavoidable. The context in each case is quite clear, however.

Chapter VIII

1. See (46) for Bohm-Bawerk.

2. Wicksteed's article "Das Kapital: A Criticism", along with Shaw's comment and Wicksteed's rejoinder, are published in (50) pp.705-733. For the importance of Wicksteed's criticism, see the essay on Victorian critics of Marx in (17).

3. Hyndman's polemical answer under the title "The Final Futility of Final Utility" was in (18).

4. For Bortkiewicz see (46) and (7). The discussion here is based mainly on (46).

5.   References to the von Neumann and related articles are given in the bibliography of (42).

6.   See the reference to Winternitz in (42).

7.   See (41).

8.   See (42).

9.   See (37).

Chapter IX

1.   This discussion is based, of course, on *Capital*, Vol. III.   See also (45) for a comprehensive account of the Marx and Bortkiewicz solutions. Meek in (35) summarises the Winternitz solution and compares it with that of Bortkiewicz. Our notation is slightly different from that of Sweezy in (45).

2.   Joan Robinson in her early work on Marx (39) took this view. For a summary of similar views see (35). Professor Robinson's views today are no longer the same.

Chapter X

1.   For references see footnote 4 to Chapter VIII.

2.   We return to this point again when discussing the Law of Falling Rate of Profit and the difficulties involved in testing it. (See Chapters XVII and XVIII). Many would not agree with drawing so sharp a difference. Meek for example in the Introduction to (35) takes the view that normalisation rules are arbitrary.

Chapter XI

1.   Professor Samuelson goes further and says that the problem arises only due to the persistence of Marxists with an erroneous and un-necessary set of value equations. See (42).

2.   See especially (16) and (11), which is also included in (3).

3.   Many would disagree. For instance, Morishima in the concluding chapter of (37) thinks that equal rates of exploitation are a vital part of Marx's system. I return to this problem in the concluding chapter.

Chapter XII

1.   Leontieff was a student of Bortkiewicz who was familiar with the work of Dimitriev and Tugan-Baranowsky as is evident from (7).

Chapter XIII

1.   Constancy of r and g_i over time is indeed contrary to Marx's own discussion of the falling rate of profit in Vol. III and to his discussion of the absolute and relative rates of surplus value in Vol. I of *Capital*. This again illustrates how Marx often made assumptions for arithmetical convenience which were in no way a part of his general model. This has obvious reference to my interpretation regarding the inter-Departmental equality of the rate of surplus value. (See footnote 3 to Chapter VI) above.

2.   The reference here and in subsequent discussion is to (28).

3.   (28), p.343.

Chapter XIV

1. (28)

2. Rosa Luxemburg quotes Marx extensively on this point in (28).

Chapter XV

1. The material in this Chapter comes from Section 3 on "The Historical Conditions of Accumulation" in (28).

Chapter XVI

1. *Capital* III/48/797.

2. The theory of the investment schedule is much too large an area to go into here. The treatments given by Wicksell, Keynes, Kalecki and Irving Fisher, among others, are all different. For a recent discussion of the continuing debate see (13), Chapter 8, pp.211-246.

3. For a reference to some of these models see the citation in footnote 4 below.

4. (37) Chapter 10, pp.117-128.

Chapter XVII

1. See (2) and (15) which are discussed in the concluding Chapter.

2. See (48) for the argument that Marx took over the law of the falling rate of profit from other classical writers though it contradicts other aspects of his work.

3. In recent years in the UK there have been recurring complaints by industrialists that the rate of profit has been falling. See (15) for a statistical investigation.

Chapter XVIII

1. The reference here is to (14).

2. I am using the expressions 'value of product' and 'value added' in their statistical and not in their Marxian sense. The symbols used in this Chapter have been defined previously in our discussion of the Transformation problem.

3. (14) p.147.

4. Glyn and Sutcliffe in (15) take a straightforward accounting approach and do not explicitly relate the rate of profit to the Marxian concept.

Chapter XIX

1. For an account of the discussion of many of these people's work, see Section 2 of (28) and Chapter 11 of (45).

2. Such a view was taken, for example, by Klein in (22).

3. This view has been advanced by Aubrey Jones in (19).

4. Page numbers are cited in the text itself beside each quotation. The full reference is in the bibliography.

5. The Okun gap, known after Professor A. Okun, is the difference between GNP at full employment and the actual GNP at any time. It is now a widely-used operational concept in US economic policy.

6. Sweezy has debated many of these points in a recent issue of *The Bulletin of the Conference of Socialist Economists*. See (47) for the full reference.

7. Once again quotations are cited directly as in the case of Baran and Sweezy above.

8. See (26).

9. See (43).

10. This view has been taken by C. von Weiszacker in (49).

11. (42), footnote 5.

12. See (15).

QUOTATIONS FROM "CAPITAL"

In each case the Roman numeral indicates volume, the next set
of numbers the chapter and the last the page of the citation.
Many of these quotations include superscripts for footnotes but
these have been omitted except when Marx is quoting from another
source, when this information is included at the end of the
quotation. The editions of *Capital* used are as follows:

Capital Vol. I (Translated from the Third German edition by
Samuel Moore and Edward Aveling; edited by Friedrich Engels:
Encyclopaedia Britannica Inc., Great Books of the Western World,
Vol.50, Chicago and London).

Capital Vol. II (Foreign Languages Publishing House, Moscow, 1957)

Capital Vol. III (Foreign Languages Publishing House, Moscow, 1962)

In a few cases, words are put in { } to elucidate the meaning.
Interpolations in parentheses are in the original.

(1)   *Labour Time*

The labour time socially necessary is that required to produce an
article under the normal conditions of production, and with the
average degree of skill and intensity prevalent at the time.
I/1/15

(2)   *Things and Commodities*

A thing can be a use-value, without having value. This is the
case when its utility to man is not due to labour. Such are air,
virgin soil, natural meadows, etc. A thing can be useful, and
the product of human. labour, without being a commodity. Whoever
directly satisfies his wants with the produce of his own labour
creates, indeed, use-values, but not commodities. In order to
produce the latter, he must not only produce use-values, but use-
values for others, social use-values. (And not only just "for
others". The medieval peasant produced grain for feudal dues and
for the tithe. But this grain did not become a commodity merely
because it was produced for others. In order to become a commodity, the product must be transferred *by exchange* to the person
whom it will serve as use-value). I/1/16 Interpolation by
Engels.

(3)   *The Commodity Form*

Whence, then arises, the enigmatical character of the product of
labour as soon as it assumes the form of commodities? Clearly
from this form itself. The equality of all sorts of human labour
is expressed objectively by their products all being equally
valued; the measure of the expenditure of labour power by the
duration of that expenditure takes the form of the quantity of
value of the products of labour; and finally, the mutual relations
of the producers, within which the social character of their labour
affirms itself, take the form of a social relation between the
products. I/1/31

(4)   *Fetishism*

There is a physical relation between physical things. But it is
different with commodities. There the existence of the things *qua*
commodities, and the value relation between the products of labour
which stamps them as commodities, have absolutely·no connection
with their physical properties and with the material relations
arising therefrom. There it is a definite social relation between
men that assumes, in their eyes, the fantastic form of a relation
between things. ....This I call the *fetishism* which attaches
itself to the products of labour, so soon as they are produced
as commodities, and which is, therefore, inseparable from the
production of commodities. I/1/31

(5) *Dual Value Form*

This division of a product into a useful thing and a value becomes practically important only when exchange has acquired such an extension that useful articles are produced for the purpose of being exchanged, and their character as values has therefore to be taken into account, beforehand, during production. I/1/32

(6) *The Commodity Mode and its Mystery*

The categories of bourgeois economy consist of such like forms. They are forms of thought expressing with social validity the conditions and relations of a definite, historically determined mode of production, viz: the production of commodities. The whole mystery of commodities, all magic and necromancy that surrounds the products of labour as long as they take the form of commodities, vanishes, therefore, as soon as we come to other forms of production. I/1/33

(7) *European Middle Ages: Relations of Production*

Here, instead of the independent man, we find everyone dependent - serfs and lords, vassals and suzerain, laymen and clergy. Personal dependence here characterizes the social relations of production just as much as it does the other spheres of life organised on the basis of that production. But for the very reason that personal dependence forms the groundwork of society, there is no necessity for labour and its products to assume a fantastic form different from their reality. They take the shape, in the transactions of society, of services in kind and payments in kind. Here the particular and natural form of labour, and not, as in a society based on production of commodities, its general abstract form, is the immediate social form of labour. Compulsory labour is just as properly measured by time as commodity-producing labour; but every serf knows that what he expends in the service of his lord is a definite quantity of his own personal labour power. I/1/34

(8) *Mode of Production*

The mode of production in which the product takes the form of a commodity, or is produced directly for exchange, is the most general and most embryonic form of bourgeois production. I/1/37

(9) *Surplus Value*

The exact form of this process is therefore $M - C - M'$ where $M' = M + \Delta M$ = the original sum advanced, plus an increment. This increment or excess over the original value I call *surplus value*. The value originally advanced, therefore, not only remains intact while in circulation, but adds to itself a surplus value or expands itself. It is this movement that converts it into capital. I/4/71

130

(10) *Exchange*

With reference, therefore, to use-value, there is good ground for saying that "exchange is transaction at which both sides gain." It is otherwise with exchange value. I/5/74 (Marx is quoting Destutt de Tracy).

(11) *Exchange begets no value*

Turn and twist then as we may, the fact remains unaltered. If equivalents are exchanged, no surplus value results, and if non-equivalents are exchanged, still no surplus value. Circulation, or the exchange of commodities begets no value. I/5/77

(12) *Crisis*

No one can sell unless someone else purchases. But no one is forthwith bound to purchase because he has just sold.... If the interval in time between the two complementary phases of the complete metamorphosis of a commodity becomes too great, if the split between the sale and the purchase becomes too pronounced, the intimate connection between them, their oneness, asserts itself by producing a crisis. I/3/52

(13) *Source of surplus value*

The change of value that occurs in the case of money intended to be converted into capital cannot take place in the money itself, since, in its function of means of purchase and of payment, it does no more than realize the price of the commodity it buys or pays for; and, as hard cash, it is value petrified, never varying. Just as little can it originate in the second act of circulation, the resale of the commodity, which does no more than transform the article from its bodily form back again into its money form. The change must, therefore, take place in the commodity bought by the first act, M - C, but not in its value, for equivalents are exchanged and the commodity is paid for at its full value. We are, therefore, forced to the conclusion that the change originates in the use-value, as such, of the commodity, i.e. in its consumption. In order to be able to extract value from the consumption of a commodity, our friend, moneybags, must be so lucky as to find, within the sphere of circulation, in the market, a commodity whose use-value possesses the peculiar property of being a source of value, whose actual consumption, therefore, is itself an embodiment of labour, and, consequently, a creation of value. The possessor of money does find on the market such a special commodity in capacity for labour or labour power. I/3/79

(14) *Labour Power*

By *labour power* or *capacity for labour* is to be understood the
aggregate of those mental and physical capabilities existing in
a human being which he exercises whenever he produces a use-value
of any description. I/6/79.

(15) *Sale of Labour Power*

....{L}abour power can appear upon the market as a commodity only
if, and in so far as, its possessor, the individual whose labour
power it is, offers it for sale, or sells it, as a commodity.
In order that he may be able to do this, he must have it at his
disposal, must be the untramelled owner of his capacity for labour,
i.e. of his person. He and the owner of money meet in the market
and deal with each other as on the basis of equal rights, with
this difference alone, that one is buyer, the other seller; both
therefore, equal in the eyes of the law. The continuance of this
relation demands that the owner of the labour power should sell
it only for a definite period, for if he were to sell it rump and
stump, once for all, he would be selling himself, converting himself from a free man into a slave, from an owner of a commodity
into a commodity. I/6/79

(16) *Free Labour*

For the conversion of his money into capital, therefore, the
owner of money must meet in the market with the free labourer,
free in the double sense; that as a free man he can dispose of
his labour power as his own commodity, and that, on the other
hand, he has no other commodity for sale, is short of everything
necessary for the realization of his labour power. I/6/80

(17) *Historical Basis of the Category of Free Labourer*

One thing, however, is clear - Nature does not produce on the one
side owners of money, or commodities, and on the other men possess-
ing nothing but their own labour power. This relation has no
natural basis, neither is its social basis one that is common to
all historical periods. It is clearly the result of a past historical development, the product of many economic revolutions, of
the extinction of a whole series of older forms of social production.

So, too, the economic categories, already discussed by us, bear
the stamp of history. Definite historical conditions are necessary, that a product may become a commodity. I/6/80

(18) *Historical Conditions for the Existence of Capital*

It is otherwise with capital. The historical conditions of its existence are by no means given with the mere circulation of money and commodities. It can spring into life only when the owner of the means of production and subsistence meets in the market with the free labourer selling his labour power. I/6/81.

(19) *Value of Labour Power*

The value of labour power is determined as in the case of every other commodity by the labour time necessary for the production, and consequently also the reproduction, of this special article. So far as it has value, it represents no more than a definite quantity of the average labour of society incorporated in it. Labour power exists only as a capacity, or power of the living individual. Its production consequently presupposes his existence. I/6/81

(20) *Consumption of Labour Power is Production of Surplus Value*

We now know how the value paid by the purchaser to the possessor of this peculiar commodity, labour power is determined. The use value which the former gets in exchange manifests itself only in the actual usufruct, in the consumption of the labour power. The money owner buys everything necessary for this purpose, such as raw material, in the market, and pays for it at its full value. The consumption of labour power is at one and the same time the production of commodities and of surplus value. The consumption of labour power is completed, as in the case of every other commodity, outside the limits of the market or of the sphere of circulation. I/6/83

(21) *The Sphere of Exchange*

This sphere that we are deserting, within whose boundaries the sale and purchase of labour power goes on, is in fact a very Eden of the innate rights of man. There alone rule freedom, equality, property and Bentham. Freedom, because both buyer and seller of a commodity, say of labour power, are constrained only by their own free will. They contract as free agents, and the agreement they come to is both the form in which they give legal expression to their common will. Equality, because each enters into relation with the other, as with a simple owner of commodities and they exchange equivalent for equivalent. Property, because each disposes only of what is his own. And Bentham, because each looks only to himself. The only force that brings them together and puts them in relation with each other is the selfishness, the gain and the private interest of each. I/6/83-84

(22) *Why Labour Power is a Source of Surplus Value*

The value of a day's labour power amounts to 3 shillings, because on our assumption half a day's labour is embodied in that quantity of labour power, i.e. because the means of subsistence that are daily required for the production of labour power cost half a day's labour. But the past labour that it can call into action, the daily cost of maintaining it and its daily expenditure in work are two totally different things. The former determines the exchange value of the labour power, the latter is its use-value. The fact that half a day's labour is necessary to keep the labourer alive during 24 hours does not in any way prevent him from working a whole day. Therefore the value of labour power and the value which that labour power creates in the labour process are two entirely different magnitudes; and this difference between the two values was what the capitalist had in view when he was purchasing the labour power. The useful qualities that labour power possesses and by virtue of which it makes yarn or boots were to him nothing more than a *conditio sine qua non*; for in order to create value labour must be expended in a useful manner. What really influenced him was the specific use value which this commodity possesses of being *a source not only of value but of more value than it has itself*. This is the special service that the capitalist expects from labour power, and in this transaction he acts in accordance with the "eternal laws" of the exchange of commodities. The seller of labour power, like the seller of any other commodity, realizes its exchange value and parts with its use value. He cannot take the one without giving the other. I/7/93

(23) *Surplus Labour in Different Modes of Production*

The essential difference between the various economic forms of society, between, for instance, a society based on slave labour and one based on wage labour, lies only in the mode in which this surplus labour is in each case extracted from the actual producer, the labourer. I/9/105

(24) *Limits to Surplus Labour in Non-Capitalist Forms*

It is, however, clear that in any given economic formation of society, where not the exchange value but the use-value of the product predominates, surplus labour will be limited by a given set of wants which may be greater or less, and that here no boundless thirst for surplus labour arises from the nature of the production itself. I/10/113

(25) *Length of the Working Day is Determined by Class Struggle*

We see, then, that apart from extremely elastic bounds, the nature of the exchange of commodities itself imposes no limit to the working day, no limit to surplus labour. The capitalist maintains his rights as a purchaser when he tries to make the working day as long as possible, and to make, whenever possible, two working days out of one. On the other hand, the peculiar nature of the commodity sold implies a limit to its consumption by the purchaser, and the labourer maintains his right as a seller when he wishes to reduce the working day to one of definite normal duration. There is here, therefore, an antinomy, right against right, both equally bearing the seal of the law of exchanges. Between equal right, force decides. Hence is it that, in the history of capitalist production, the determination of what is a working day presents itself as the result of a struggle, a struggle between collective capital, i.e. the class of capitalists, and collective labour, i.e. the working class. I/10/113.

(26) *Slave Labour in Capitalist Mode of Production* (Negro labour in the Southern USA)

But as soon as people, whose production still moves within the lower forms of slave-labour, corvée-labour, etc., are drawn into the whirlpool of an international market dominated by the capitalist mode of production, the sale of their products for export becoming their principal interest, the civilised horrors of overwork are grafted on the barbaric horrors of slavery, serfdom, etc. Hence, the negro labour in the southern states of the American Union preserved something of a patriarchal character, so long as production was chiefly directed to immediate local consumption. But in proportion, as the export of cotton became of vital interest to these states, the overworking of the negro and sometimes the using up of his life in seven years of labour became a factor in a calculated and calculating system. It was no longer a question of obtaining from him a certain quantity of useful products. It was now a question of production of surplus labour itself. I/10/114

(27) *The Struggle for the Normal Working Day*

The changes in the material mode of production, and the corresponding changes in the social relations of the producers, gave rise first to an extravagance beyond all bounds, and then, in opposition to this, called forth a control on the part of the society which legally limits, regulates and makes uniform the working day and its pauses. I/10/144

The creation of a normal working day is, therefore, the product of a protracted civil war, more or less dissembled, between the capitalist class and the working class. I/10/145

(28) *Productivity of Labour and Relative Surplus Value*

In order to effect a fall in the value of labour power, the increase in the productiveness of labour must seize upon those branches of industry whose products determine the value of labour power and, consequently, either belong to the class of customary means of subsistence or are capable of supplying the place of these means. But the value of a commodity is determined not only by the quantity of labour which the labourer directly bestows upon that commodity, but also by the labour contained in the means of production.... Hence, a fall in the value of labour power is also brought about by an increase in the productiveness of labour, and by a corresponding cheapening of commodities in those industries which supply the instruments of labour and the raw material that form the material elements of constant capital required for producing the necessaries of life. I/12/153-154

The value of commodities is in inverse ratio to the productiveness of labour. And so, too, is the value of labour power, because it depends on the values of commodities. Relative surplus value is, on the contrary, directly proportional to that productiveness. I/12/155-156.

Hence there is immanent in capital an inclination and constant tendency to heighten the productiveness of labour in order to cheapen commodities, and by such cheapening to cheapen the labourer himself. I/12/156

(29) *Co-operation Among Labourers in the Capitalist Mode*

....{W}age labourers cannot co-operate unless they are employed simultaneously by the same capital, the same capitalist and unless, therefore, their labour powers are bought simultaneously by him. I/13/160

The work of directing, superintending and adjusting becomes one of the functions of capital from the moment that the labour under the control of capital becomes co-operative. Once a function of capital, it acquires special characteristics.

The directing motive, the end and aim of capitalist production, is to extract the greatest amount of surplus value and, consequently, to exploit labour power to the greatest possible extent. As the number of the co-operating labourers increases, so, too, does their resistance to the domination of capital and with it the necessity for capital to overcome this resistance by counter-pressure. The control exercised by the capitalist is not only a special function, due to the nature of the social labour process, and peculiar to that process, but it is, at the same time, a function of the exploitation of a social labour process and is consequently rooted in the unavoidable antagonism between the exploiter and the living and labouring raw material he exploits. I/13/161

(30) *Functions of the Capitalist*

When comparing the mode of production of isolated peasants and artisans with production by slave labour, the political economist counts this labour of superintendence among the *faux frais* of production. But, when considering the capitalist mode of production, he, on the contrary, treats the work of control made necessary by the co-operative character of the labour process as identical with the different work of control, necessitated by the capitalist character of that process and the antagonism of interest between capitalist character of that process and the antagonism of interest between capitalist and labourer. It is not because he is a leader of industry that a man is a capitalist; on the contrary, he is a leader of industry because he is a capitalist. The leadership of industry is an attribute of capital, just as in feudal times the functions of general and judge were attributes of landed property. I/13/162.

(31) *Political Economy as Influenced by Manufacture*

Political economy, which as an independent science first sprang into being during the period of manufacture, views the social division of labour only from the standpoint of manufacture and sees in it only the means of producing more commodities with a given quantity of labour, and, consequently, of cheapening commodities and hurrying on the accumulation of capital. In most striking contrast with the accentuation of quantity and exchange value is the attitude of the writers of classical antiquity, who hold exclusively by quality and use-value. I/14/178

(32) *Productive Labour as a Social Relation*

Hence the notion of a productive labourer implies not merely a relation between work and useful effect, between labourer and product of labour, but also a specific social relation of production, a relation that has sprung up historically and stamps the labourer as the direct means of creating surplus value. To be a productive labourer is, therefore, not a piece of luck but a misfortune. I/16/251.

(33) *Determinants of Productiveness of Labour*

Apart from the degree of development, greater or less, in the form of social production, the productiveness of labour is fettered by physical conditions. These are all referable to the constitution of man himself (race, etc.) and to surrounding nature. The external physical conditions fall into two great economic classes: (1) natural wealth in the means of subsistence, i.e. a fruitful soil, waters teeming with fish, etc. and (2), natural wealth in the instruments of labour, such as waterfalls, navigable rivers, wood, metal, coal, etc. I/16/253

(34) *Changes in the Value of Labour Power*

The value of labour power is determined by the value of a given
quantity of necessaries. It is the value and not the mass of
these necessaries that varies with the productiveness of labour.
It is, however, possible that, owing to an increase of productiveness, both the labourer and the capitalist may simultaneously
be able to appropriate a greater quantity of these necessaries
without any change in the price of labour power or in surplus
value... Although labour power would be unchanged in price, it
would be above its value. If, however, the price of labour has
fallen, not to {1s 6d}, the lowest point consistent with its new
value, but to {2s 10d or 2s 6d}, still this lower price would
represent an increased mass of necessaries. In this way it is
possible, with an increasing productiveness of labour, for the
price of labour power to keep on falling and yet this fall to be
accompanied by a constant growth in the mass of the labourer's
means of subsistence. I/17/258

(35) *Determinants of Surplus Value and Price of Labour Power*

I assume: (1) that commodities are sold at their value; (2) that
the price of labour power rises occasionally above its value, but
never sinks below it.

On this assumption, we have seen that the relative magnitudes of
surplus value and of price of labour power are determined by
three circumstances (1) the length of the working day, or the
extensive magnitude of labour; (2) the normal intensity of labour,
its intensive magnitude, whereby a given quantity of labour is
expended in a given time; (3) the productiveness of labour, whereby
the same quantum of labour yields, in a given time, a greater or
less quantum of product, dependent on the degree of development in
the conditions of production.

. . . . . .

On these assumptions the value of labour power and the magnitude
of surplus value are determined by three laws.
(1) A working day of given length always creates the same amount
of value, no matter how the productiveness of labour and, with it,
the mass of the product, and the price of each single commodity
produced, may vary.
(2) Surplus value and the value of labour power vary in opposite
directions. A variation in the productiveness of labour, its
increase or diminution, causes a variation in the opposite direction in the value of labour power, and in the same direction in
surplus value.
(3) Increase or diminution in surplus value is always consequent
on, and never the cause of, the corresponding dimunution or
increase in the value of labour power. I/17/256-257

(36) *The Value of Labour and the Value of Labour Power*

That which comes directly face to face with the possessor of
money on the market is in fact not labour, but the labourer.
What the latter sells is his labour power. As soon as his labour
actually begins it has already ceased to belong to him; it can
therefore no longer be sold by him. Labour is the substance and
the immanent measure of value, *but has itself no value*.

In the expression "value of labour", the idea of value is not only
completely obliterated, but actually reversed. It is an expression as imaginary as the value of the earth . These imaginary
expressions arise, however, from the relations of production themselves. They are categories for the phenomiral forms of essential
relations. That in their appearance things often represent themselves in inverted form is pretty well known in every science
except political economy. I/19/265

(37) *The Value of Labour as Seen by Economists*

What economists call *value of labour* is in fact the value of
labour power as it exists in the personality of the labourer,
which is different from its function, labour, as a machine is from
the work it performs. Occupied with the difference between the
market price of labour and its so-called value, with the relation
of this value to the rate of profit, and to the values of the
commodities produced by means of labour, etc., they never discovered that the course of the analysis had led not only from the
market prices of labour to its presumed value, but had led to the
resolution of this value of labour itself into the value of labour
power. Classical economy never arrived at a consciousness of the
results of its own analysis; it accepted uncritically the categories "value of labour", "natural price of labour", etc., as
final and as adequate expressions for the value relation under
consideration and was thus led, as will be seen later, into
inextricable confusion and contradiction, while it offered to the
vulgar economists a secure basis of operations for their shallow-
ness, which on principle worships appearances only. I/19/265-266

(38) *The Value of Labour is Greater than the Value of Labour Power*

As the value of labour is only an irrational expression for the
value of labour power, it follows, of course, that the value of
labour must always be less than the value it produces, for the
capitalist always makes labour power work longer than is necessary
for the reproduction of its own value... Thus we have a result
absurd at first sight - that labour which creates a value of 6s.
possesses a value of 3s. I/19/266

(39) *The Wage Form*

The wage form thus extinguishes every trace of the division of th
working day into necessary labour and surplus labour into paid an
unpaid labour. All labour appears as paid labour. In the corvee
the labour of the worker for himself, and his compulsory labour
for his lord, differ in space and time in the clearest possible
way. In slave labour, even that part of the working day in whic
the slave is only replacing the value of his own means of existen
in which, therefore, in fact, he works for himself alone, appears
as labour for his master. All the slave's labour appears as unpa
labour. In wage labour, on the contrary, even surplus labour, or
unpaid labour, appears as paid. There the property relation conceals the labour of the slave for himself; here the money relati
conceals the unrequited labour of the wage labourer.

Hence we may understand the decisive importance of the transforma
tion of value and price of labour power into the form of wages, o
into the value and price of labour itself. This phenominal form,
which makes the actual relation invisible and, indeed, shows the
direct opposite of that relation, forms the basis of all the
juridical notions of both labourer and capitalist, of all the
mystifications of the capitalistic mode of production, of all its
illusions as to liberty, of all the apologetic shifts of the
vulgar economists. I/19/266

(40) *The Capitalist and the Value of Labour*

He {the capitalist} wishes to receive as much labour as possible
for as little money as possible. Practically, therefore, the onl
thing that interests him is the difference between the price of
labour power and the value which its function creates. But, then
he tries to buy all commodities as cheaply as possible and always
accounts for his profit by simple cheating, by buying under and
selling over the value. Hence, he never comes to see that, if su
a thing as the value of labour really existed and he really paid
this value, no capital would exist; his money would not be turne
into capital. I/19/267

(41) *The Wage Form and the Value Substance*

For the rest, in respect to the phenominal form, "value and price
of labour", or "wages", as contrasted with the essential relation
manifested therein (viz. the value and price of labour power), th
same difference holds that in respect to all phenomena and their
hidden substrata. The former appears directly and spontaneously
as current modes of thought; the latter must first be discovered
by science. Classical political economy nearly touches the true
relation of things without, however, consciously formulating it.
This it cannot, so long as it sticks in its bourgeois skin.
I/19/267

(42) *Division of Surplus Value*

The capitalist who produces surplus value - i.e. who extracts
unpaid labour directly from the labourers, and fixes it in
commodities - is, indeed, the first appropriator, but by no means
the ultimate owner, of this surplus value. He has to share it
with capitalists, with landowners, etc., who fulfil other functions
in the complex of social production. Surplus value, therefore,
splits up into various parts. Its fragments fall to various categories of persons and take various forms, independent the one of
the other, such as profit, interest, merchants' profit, rent, etc.
I/Introduction to Ch. 23/279.

(43) *Converting Money into Capital*

We saw, in Chapter IV, that in order to convert money into capital
something more is required than the production and circulation of
commodities. We saw that, on the one side, the possessor of value
or money, on the other, the possessor of the value of creating
substance; on the one side, the possessor of the means of production and subsistence, on the other, the possessor of nothing but
labour power, must confront one another as buyer and seller. The
separation of labour from its product, of subjective labour power
from the objective conditions of labour, was therefore the real
foundation in fact and the starting point of capitalist production.
I/23/282.

(44) *Creation of Capital and Perpetuation of the Labourer*

But that which at first was but a starting point becomes, by the
mere continuity of the process, by simple reproduction, the peculiar
result, constantly renewed and perpetuated, of capitalist production.
On the one hand, the process of production incessantly converts
material wealth into capital, into means of creating more wealth
and means of enjoyment for the capitalist. On the other hand, the
labourer, on quitting the process, is what he was on entering it,
a source of wealth, but devoid of all means of making that wealth
his own. Since, before entering the process, his own labour has
already been alienated from himself by the sale of his labour power,
has been appropriated by the capitalist and incorporated with
capital, it must, during the process, be realised in a product that
does not belong to him. Since the process of production is also
the process by which the capitalist consumes labour power, the
product of the labourer is incessantly converted, not only into
commodities, but into capital, into value that sucks up the value-
creating power, into means of subsistence that buy the person of
the labourer, into means of production that command the producers.
The labourer, therefore, constantly produces material, objective
wealth, but in the form of capital of an alien power that dominates
and exploits him; and the capitalist as constantly produces labour
power, but in the form of a subjective source of wealth, separated
from the objects in and by which it can alone be realized; in short
he produces the labourer, but as a wage labourer. This incessant

reproduction, this perpetuation of the labourer, is the *sine qua non* of capitalist production. I/23/282

(45) *The Capitalist and Accumulation of Capital*

But, so far as he {the capitalist} is personified capital, it is not values in use and the enjoyment of them, but exchange value and its augmentation, that spur him into action. Fanatically bent on making value expand itself, he ruthlessly forces the human race to produce for production's sake; he thus forces the develop ment of the productive powers of society and creates those materia conditions which alone can form the real basis of a higher form of society, a society in which the full and free development of every individual forms the ruling principle. Only as personified capita is the capitalist respectable. As such, he shares with the miser the passion for wealth as wealth. But that which in the miser is a mere idiosyncracy is in the capitalist the effect of the social mechanism of which he is but one of the wheels. Moreover, the development of capitalist production makes it constantly necessary to keep increasing the amount of capital laid out in a given indus trial undertaking, and competition makes the immanent laws of capitalist production to be felt by each individual capitalist as external coercive laws. It compels him to keep constantly extend- ing his capital, in order to preserve it, but extend it he cannot except by means of progressive accumulation. I/24/292-293

(46) *Rising Labour Productivity and Rising Real Wage*

But, hand-in-hand with the increasing productivity of labour goes, as we have seen, the cheapening of the labourer, therefore a higher rate of surplus value, even when the real wages are rising. The latter never rise proportionally to the productive power of labour. I/24/299

(47) *Improvement in Machinery*, etc. ('Embodied' and 'Disembodied' Technical Change)

The development of the productive power of labour reacts also on the original capital already engaged in the process of production. A part of the functioning constant capital consists of instruments of labour, such as machinery, etc; which are not consumed and therefore not reproduced or replaced by new ones of the same kind until after long periods of time. But every year a part of these instruments of labour perishes or reaches the limit of its produc- tive function. It reaches, therefore, in that year, the time for its periodical reproduction, for its replacement by new ones of the same kind. If the productiveness of labour has, during the using up of these instruments of labour, increased (and it develops con- tinually with the uninterrupted advance of science and technology) more efficient and (considering their increased efficiency) cheaper machines, tools, apparatus, etc. replace the old. The old capital

142

is reproduced in a more productive form, apart from the constant detail improvements in the instruments of labour already in use. The other part of the constant capital, raw material and auxiliary substances, is constantly reproduced in less than a year; these produced by agriculture, for the most part, annually. Every introduction of improved methods, therefore, works almost simultaneously on the new capital and on that already in action. ....Of course, this development of productive power is accompanied by a partial depreciation of functioning capital so far as this depreciation makes itself acutely felt in competition, the burden falls on the labourer, in the increased exploitation of whom the capitalist looks for his indemnification. I/24/299.

(48) *Rising Real Wages and Accumulation*

Wages, as we have seen, by their very nature, always imply the performance of a certain quantity of unpaid labour on the part of the labourer. Altogether, irrespective of the case of a rise in wages with a falling price of labour, etc., such an increase only means at best a quantitative diminution of the unpaid labour that the worker has to supply. The diminution can never reach the point at which it would threaten the system itself. Apart from violent conflicts as to the rate of wages (and Adam Smith has already shown that in such a conflict, taken on the whole, the master is always master), a rise in the price of labour resulting from accumulation of capital implies the following alternative: either the price of labour keeps on rising, because its rise does not interfere with the progress of accumulation... In this case it is evident that a diminution in the unpaid labour in no way interferes with the extension of the domain of capital. Or, on the other hand, accumulation slackens in consequence of the rise in the price of labour, because the stimulus of gain is blunted. The rate of accumulation lessens; but with lessening, the primary cause of that lessening vanishes, i.e., the disproportion between capital and exploitable labour power. The mechanism of the process of capitalist production removes the very obstacle that it temporarily creates. The price of labour falls again to a level corresponding with the needs of the self expansion of capital, whether the level be below, the same as, or above the one which was normal before the rise of wages took place. I/25/306.

(49) *Accumulation and Crises*

To put it mathematically, the rate of accumulation is the independent, not the dependent, variable; the rate of wages the dependent, not the independent, variable. Thus, when the industrial cycle is in the phase of crisis, a general fall in the price of commodities is expressed as a rise in the value of money and in the phase of prosperity, a general rise in the price of commodities, as a fall in the value of money. The so-called currency school concludes from this that with high prices too little, with low prices too much money is in circulation. Their ignorance and complete misunderstanding of facts are worthily paralleled by the

143

economists, who interpret the above phenomena of accumulation by saying that there are now too few, now too many, wage labourers. I/25/307.

(50) *Movement of Wages and the Industrial Cycle*

Taking them as a whole, the general movement of wages are exclusively regulated by the expansion and contraction of the industrial reserve army, and these again correspond to the periodic changes of the industrial cycle. They are, therefore, not determined by the variations of the absolute number of the working population, but by the varying proportions in which the working class is divided into active and reserve army, by the increase or diminution in the relative amount of the surplus population, by the extent to which it is now absorbed, now set free. I/25/315

(51) *Primitive Accumulation*

We have seen how money is changed into capital; how, through capital, surplus value is made and from surplus value more capital. But the accumulation of capital presupposes surplus value, surplus value presupposes capitalistic production; capitalistic production presupposes the pre-existence of considerable masses of capital and of labour power in the hands of producers of commodities. The whole movement, therefore, seems to turn in a vicious circle, out of which we can only get by supposing a primitive accumulation. (The "previous accumulation" of Adam Smith) preceding capitalistic accumulation; an accumulation not the result of the capitalist mode of production, but its starting point. I/26/354.

(52) *The Methods of Primitive Accumulation*

In the tender annals of political economy, the idyllic reigns from time immemorial. Right and "labour" were from all time the sole means of enrichment, the present year, of course, always excepted. As a matter of fact, the methods of primitive accumulation are anything but idyllic.

(53) *The Process of Primitive Accumulation*

The process, therefore, that clears the way for the capitalist system can be none other than the process which takes away from the labourer the possession of his means of production, a process that transforms, on the one hand, the social means of subsistence and of production into capital, on the other, the immediate producers into wage labourers. The so-called primitive accumulation, therefore, is nothing else than the historical process of divorcing the producer from the means of production. I/26/354-355

144

(54) *The Role of Force in Primitive Accumulation and in Capitalism*

The dull compulsion of economic relations compels the subjection of the labourer to the capitalist. Direct force, outside economic conditions, is of course still used, but only exceptionally. In the ordinary run of things, the labourer can be left to the "natural laws of production", i.e. to his dependence on capital, a dependence springing from, and guaranteed in perpetuity by, the conditions of production themselves. It is otherwise during the historic genesis of capitalist production. The bourgeoisie, at its rise, wants and uses the power of the state to "regulate" wages, i.e. to force them within the limits suitable for surplus value making, to lengthen the working day and to keep the labourer himself in the normal degree of dependence. This is an essential element of the so-called primitive accumulation. I/28/366

(55) *Force*

Force is the midwife of every old society pregnant with a new one. It is itself an economic power. I/31/372

(56) *Money and Money Capital*

Capital in the form of money-capital is in a state in which it can perform the functions of money, in the present case the functions of a universal means of purchase and universal means of payment. ...This capacity is not due to the fact that money capital is capital but that it is money.

On the other hand capital-value in the form of money cannot perform any other functions but those of money . What turns the money functions into functions of capital is the definite role they play in the movement of capital, and therefore also this inter-relation of the stage in which these functions are performed with the other stages of the circuit of capital. Take, for instance, the case with which we are here dealing. Money is here converted into commodities, the combination of which represents the bodily form of productive capital, and this form already contains latently, potentially, the result of the process of capitalist production. II/1/26

(57) *M - L: Capital in the Purchase of Labour Power*

M - L is the characteristic moment in the transformation of money-capital into productive capital, because it is the essential condition for the real transformation of value advanced in the form of money into capital, into a value producing surplus value. II/1/27

(58) *M - L: Hallmark of the Money System*

M - L is regarded as the characteristic feature, the hallmark of the so-called money system, because labour there appears as the commodity of its owner, and money therefore as the buyer - hence on account of the money-relation (i.e. the sale and purchase of human activity). II/1/28.

(59) *Labour Power as a Commodity*

Once labour-power has come into the market as the commodity of its owner and its sale takes the form of payment for labour, assumes the shape of wages, its purchase and sale is no more startling than the purchase and sale of any other commodity. The characteristic thing is not that the commodity labour-power is purchasable but that labour-power appears as a commodity. II/1/28

(60) *M - L: The Exchange and the Class-Relation*

True, in the act M - L the owner of money and the owner of labour-power enter only into the relation of buyer and seller, confront one another only as money-owner and commodity-owner. In this respect they enter merely into a money relation. Yet at the same time the buyer appears also from the outset in the capacity of an owner of means of production, which are the material conditions for the productive expenditure of labour-power by its owner. In other words, these means of production are in opposition to the owner of the labour-power, being property of another. On the other hand the seller of labour faces its buyer as labour-power of another which must be made to do his bidding, must be integrated into his capital, in order that it may really become productive capital. The class relation between capitalist and wage-labourer therefore exists, is presupposed from the moment that the two face each other in act M - L (L - M on the part of the labourer). It is a purchase and sale, a money-relation, but a purchase and sale in which the buyer is assumed to be a capitalist and the seller a wage-labourer. And this relation arises out of the fact that the conditions required for the realization of labour-power, viz., means of subsistence and means of production, are separated from the owner of labour-power, being the property of another. II/1/29.

(61) *Capital as a Relation*

The capital-relation during the process of production arises only because it is inherent in the act of circulation, in the different fundamental economic conditions in which the buyer and seller confront each other in their class relation. It is not money which by its nature creates this relation; it is rather the existence of this relation which permits of the transformation of a mere money-function into a capital-function. II/1/30.

(62) _M - L: The Historical Conditions_

In order that the sale of one's own labour-power (in the form of
the sale of one's own labour or in the form of wages) may consti-
tute not an isolated phenomenon but a socially decisive premise
for the production of commodities, in order that money-capital
may therefore perform, on a social scale, the above-discussed

function $M - C < \frac{L}{MP}$ historical processes are assumed by which

the original connection of the means of production with labour-
power was dissolved - processes in consequence of which the mass
of the people, the labourers, have as non-owners, come face to
face with the non-labourers as the owners of these means of
production. II/1/31

(63) _The Production Function is Ahistorical_

Whatever the social form of production, labourers and means of
production always remain factors of it. ...For production to go
on at all they must unite. The specific manner in which this
union is accomplished distinguishes the different economic epochs
of the structure of society from one another. II/1/34

(64) _The Different Nature of Means of Production and Labour-Power_

The means of production and labour-power, in so far as they are
forms of existence of advanced capital-value, are distinguished
by the different roles assumed by them during the process of
production in the creation of value, hence also of surplus value,
into constant and variable capital. Being different components
of productive capital they are furthermore distinguished by the
fact that the means of production in the possession of the capitalist remains his capital even outside of the process of production,
while labour-power becomes the form of existence of an individual
capital only within this process. Whereas labour-power is a
commodity only in the hands of its seller, the wage-labourer, it
becomes capital only in the hands of its buyer, the capitalist
who acquires the temporary use of it.

(65) _Interruptions in the Circuit of Capital: Hoard, Idle Capacity,_
Excess Supply

Capital describes its circuit normally only so long as its various
phases pass uninterruptedly into one another. If capital stops
short in its first phase M - C, money capital assumes the rigid
form of a hoard; if it stops short in the phase of production, the
means of production lie without functioning on the one side, while
labour-power remains unemployed on the other; and if capital is
stopped short in its last phase C' - M', piles of unsold commodities accumulate and clog the flow of circulation. II/1/48

(66) *Commodity-Output and Services*

In the general formula the product of P is regarded as a material thing different from the elements of the productive capital, as an object existing apart from the process of production and having a use-form different from that of elements of production. This is always the case when the result of the productive process assumes the form of a thing even when a part of the product re-enters the resumed production as one of its elements... . But there are certain independent branches of industry in which the product of the productive process is not a new material product, is not a commodity. Among these only the communications industry, whether engaged in transportation proper, of goods and passengers, or in the mere transmission of communications, letters, telegrams, etc$_1$, is economically important. II/1/51-52.

(67) *The Process as Seen by Vulgar Economy*

And so we have premised simple reproduction, i.e. that m - c separates entirely from M - C. Since both circulations, c - m - c as well as C - M - C, belong in the circulation of commodities, so far as their general form is concerned (and for this reason do not show any value differences in their extremes); it is easy to conceive the process of capitalist production, after the manner of vulgar economy, as a mere production of commodities, of use-values designed for consumption of some sort, which the capitalist produces for no other purpose than that of getting in their place commodities with different use-values, or of exchanging them for such, as vulgar economy erroneously states. II/2/68

(68) *Ever Changing Values*

In order that the circuit may be completed normally, C' must be sold at its value and its entirety. Furthermore, C - M - C includes not merely replacement of one commodity by another, but replacement with value-relations remaining the same. We assume that this takes place here. As a matter of fact, however, the values of the means of production vary. It is precisely capitalist production to which continuous change of value-relations is peculiar, if only because of the ever changing productivity of labour that characterizes this mode of production. II/2/72

(69) *Continuous Expansion of Capital*

The entire character of capitalist production is determined by the self-expansion of the advanced capital-value, that is to say, in the first instance by the production of as much surplus-value as possible; in the second place, however, (see Vol. I Ch.24) by the production of capital, hence, by the transformation of surplus-value into capital. Accumulation, or production on an extended scale, which appears as a means of constantly more expanded production of surplus-value - hence for enrichment of the capitalist, as

his personal aim - and is comprised in the general tendency of
capitalist production, becomes, later, however, as was shown in
Book I, by virtue of its development a necessity for every individual capitalist. The constant augmentation of his capital becomes
a condition of its preservation. II/2/78-79

(70) *The Circuit of Productive Capital and Political Economy*

The general form of the movement P....P is the form of reproduction and, unlike M....M', does not indicate the self-expansion of
value as the object of the process. This form makes it therefore
so much easier for classical Political Economy to ignore the definite capitalistic form of the process of production and to depict
production as such as the purpose of this process; namely that
as much as possible must be produced and as cheaply as possible,
and that the product must be exchanged for the greatest variety
of other products, partly for the renewal of production (M - C),
partly for consumption (m - c). It is then possible to overlook
the peculiarities of money and money-capital, for M and m appear
here merely as transient media of circulation. The entire process
seems simple and natural, i.e., possesses the naturalness of a
shallow rationalism. II/3/92

(71) *Why the Circuit of Commodity Capital Appears as the General Form*

But just because the circuit C'...C' presupposes within its sphere
the existence of other industrial capital in the form of C (equal
to L + MP) - and MP comprises diverse other capitals in our case,
for instance machinery, coal, oil, etc. - it clamours to be
considered not only as the *general* form of the circuit, i.e. not
only as a social form in which every single industrial capital
(except when first invested) can be studied, hence not merely as
a form of movement common to all individual industrial capitals,
but simultaneously also as a form of movement of the sum of the
individual capitals, consequently of the aggregate capital of the
capitalist class, a movement in which that of each individual
industrial capital appears as only a partial movement which inter-
mingles with the other movements and is necessitated by them.
II/3/96-97

(72) *The Circuit of Commodity Capital as a One-Sided Conception*

In Formula III {C' - C'} commodities in the market are the continuous premise of the process of production and reproduction.
Hence, if attention is fixed exclusively on this formula all
elements of the process of production seem to originate in commodity circulation and to consist only of commodities. This one-
sided conception overlooks those elements of the process of
production which are independent of the commodity-elements.
II/3/98-99

(73) *Commodity Circuit and Quesnay*

C' - C' is the groundwork for Quesnay's *Tableau Economique* and it shows great and true discretion on his part that in contrast to M....M' (the isolatedly and rigidly retained form of the mercantile system) he selected this form and not P....P. II/3/99

(74) *Capital as a Dynamic Process*

Capital, as self-expanding value embraces not only class relations, a society of a definite character resting on the existence of labour in the form of wage-labour. It is a movement, a circuit-describing process going through various stages, which itself comprises three different forms of the circuit-describing process. Therefore, it can be understood only as motion, not as a thing at rest. II/4/105.

(75) *Individual Capital and Revolutions in Value*

The movements of capital appear as the action of some individual industrial capitalist who performs the functions of a buyer of commodities and labour, a seller of commodities, and an owner of productive capital, who therefore promotes the circuit by his activity. If social capital experiences a revolution in value the more does the automatic movement of the now independent value operate with the elemental force of a natural process against the foresight and calculation of the individual capitalist, the more does the course of normal production become subservient to abnormal speculation and the greater is the danger that threatens the existence of the individual capitals. These periodical revolutions in value therefore corroborate what they are supposed to refute, namely, that value as capital acquires independent existence, which it maintains and accentuates through its movement. II/4/105-106

(76) *Industrial Capitalism and Other Modes of Production in the World Market*

Within its process of circulation, in which industrial capital functions either as money or as commodities, the circuit of industrial capital, whether as money-capital or as commodity-capital, crosses the commodity circulation of the most diverse modes of social production, so far as they produce commodities. No matter whether commodities are the output of production based on slavery of peasants (Chinese, Indian ryots), of communes (Dutch East Indies), of state enterprises (such as existed in former epochs of Russian history on the basis of serfdom) or of half-savage hunting tribes, etc. - as commodities and money they come face to face with the money and commodities in which the industrial capital presents itself and enter as much into its circuit as into that of surplus-value borne in the commodity-capital, provided the surplus-value is spent as revenue; hence they enter into both branches of circulation of commodity-capital. The character of the process of production from which they originate is immaterial. They function

150

as commodities in the market, and as commodities they enter into the circuit of industrial capital as well as into the circulation of the surplus-value incorporated in it. It is therefore the universal character of the origin of the commodities, the existence of the market as world market, which distinguishes the process of circulation of industrial capital. II/4/109-110.

(77) *Profits as Apparent Result of Time of Circulation*

A capital's time of circulation therefore limits, generally speaking, its time of production and hence its process of genera- ting surplus value. And it limits this process in proportion to its own duration. This duration may considerably increase or decrease and hence may restrict capital's time of production in a widely varying degree. But Political Economy sees only what is *apparent*, namely the effect of the time of circulation on capital's process of the creation of surplus-value in general. It takes this negative effect for a positive one, because its consequences are positive. It clings the more tightly to this appearance since it seems to furnish proof that capital possesses a mystic source of self-expansion independent of its process of production and hence of the exploitation of labour, a spring which flows to it from the spheres of circulation. II/5/125

Cost-Price, Profits and Surplus Value: Things as they appear to the Capitalist

(78) *The Category of Cost-Price*

The category of cost-price, on the other hand, has nothing to do with the formation of commodity-value or with the process of self-explanation of capital... . The investigation will show, however, that in capitalist economics the cost-price assumes the false appearance of a category of value production itself. III/1/28

(79) *Surplus Value as a Product of all Capital, Labour as well as the Stock of Fixed Capital*

We have also seen earlier that though s, the surplus value, springs merely from a change in the value of the variable capital v and is, therefore, originally but an increment of variable capital, after the process of production is over, it nevertheless also forms an increment of c + v, the expended total capital. The formula c + (v + s), which indicates that s is produced through the conversion of a definite capital-value v advanced for labour power into a fluctuating magnitude, i.e. of a constant magnitude into a variable one, may also be represented as (c + v) + s. However, surplus value forms an increment not only of the portion of the advanced capital which goes into the self-expansion process. but also of the portion which does not go into it. In other words, it is an accretion not only to the consumed capital made good out of the cost-price of the commodity, but to all the capital invested in production. Before the production process we had a capital valued at 1680, namely 1,200 of fixed capital invested in means of production, only 20 of which go into the value of the commodity for wear and tear, plus 480 of circulating capital in materials of production and wages. After the production process we have 1,180 as the constituent element of the value of the productive capital plus a commodity capital of 600. By adding these two sums of value we find that the capitalist now has a value of 1,780. After deducting his advanced total capital of 1,680 there remains a value increment of 100. The 100 of surplus value thus form as much an increment in relation to the invested 1,680 as to its fraction of 500 expanded during production.

It is now clear to the capitalist that the increment of value springs from the productive processes undertaken with the capital, that it therefore springs from the capital itself, because it is there after the production process, while it is not there before it. As for the capital consumed in production, the surplus-value seems to spring equally from all its different elements of value consisting of means of production and labour. For all these elements contribute equally to the formation of the cost-price. III/1/34-35

Note: Marx is assuming here a 100% rate of surplus-value.

(80) *How Surplus Value Appears as Profit on Capital*

In its assumed capacity of offspring of the aggregate advanced capital, surplus-value takes the converted form of *profit*. Hence a certain value is capital when it is invested with a view to producing profit, or, there is profit because a certain value was employed as capital. Suppose profit is p. Then the formula $C = c + v + s = k + s$ turns into the formula $C = k + p$, or the value of a commodity = cost price + profit.

The profit, such as it is represented here, is thus the same as surplus-value, only in a mystified form that is none the less a necessary outgrowth of the capitalist mode of production.... Because at one pole the price of labour-power assumes the trans muted form of wages, surplus-value appears at the opposite pole in the transmuted form of profit. III/1/36

(81) *Cost-Price as a Measure of Value*

One minimal limit of the selling price of a commodity is its cost-price. If it is sold under its cost-price the expected constituent elements of productive capital cannot be fully replaced out of the selling price. If this process continues, the value of the advanced capital disappears. From this point of view alone, the capitalist is inclined to regard the cost-price as the true *inner* value of the commodity, because it is the price required for the bare conservation of his capital. But there is also this, that the cost-price of a commodity is the purchase price paid by the capitalist himself for its production, therefore, the purchase price determined by the production process itself. For this reason, the excess-value or the surplus-value realized in the sale of a commodity appears to the capitalist as an excess of its selling price over its value, instead of an excess of its value over its cost-price, so that accordingly the surplus-value incorporated in a commodity is not realized through its sale but springs out of the sale itself.   III/1/37-38

(82) *The Transformation of Surplus-Value into Profit*

The transformation of surplus-value into profit must be deduced from the transformation of the rate of surplus value into the rate of profit, not vice versa. And in fact it was rate of profit which was the historical point of departure. Surplus-value and rate of surplus-value are, relatively, the invisible and unknown essence that wants investigating, while rate of profit and therefore the appearance of surplus-value in the form of profit are revealed on the surface of the phenomenon.   III/2/42-43

The way in which surplus-value is transformed into the form of profit by way of the rate of profit is, however, a further development of the inversion of subject and object that takes place already in the process of production.   III/2/45

(83) *The Composition of Capital: Technical and Value Ratios*

By composition of capital we mean, as stated in Book I, the proportion of its active and passive components, i.e. of variable and constant capital. Two proportions enter into consideration under this heading. They are not equally important, although they may produce similar effects under certain circumstances.

The first proportion rests on a technical basis and must be regarded as given at a certain stage of development of the productive forces. A definite quantity of labour power represented by a definite number of labourers is required to produce a definite quantity of products, say, in one day, and - what is self-evident - thereby to consume productively, i.e. to set in motion, a definite quantity of means of production, machinery, raw materials, etc. A definite number of labourers corresponds to a definite quantity of means of production, and hence a definite quantity of living labour to a definite quantity of labour materialized in means of production. This proportion differs greatly in different spheres of production, and frequently, even in different branches of one and the same industry, although it may by coincidence be entirely or approximately the same in entirely separate lines of industry. This proportion forms the technical composition of capital and is the real basis of its organic composition.

However, it is also possible that this first proportion may be the same in different lines of industry provided that variable-capital is merely an index of labour-power and constant capital merely an index of the mass of means of production set in motion by this labour-power. For instance, certain work in copper and iron may require the same ratio of labour power to mass of means of production. But since copper is more expensive than iron, the value-relation between variable and constant capital is different in each case, and hence also the value composition of the two total capitals. III/8/143

(84) *Divergence Between Surplus-Value and Profit*

It is then only an accident if the surplus-value, and thus the profit, actually produced in any particular sphere of production, coincides with the profit contained in the selling price of a commodity. As a rule, surplus-value and profit and not their rates alone are then different magnitudes. At a given degree of exploitation, the mass of surplus-value produced in a particular sphere of production is then more important for the aggregate profit of social capital, and thus for the capitalist class in general, than for the individual capitalist in any specific branch of production. It is of importance for the latter only in so far as the quantity of surplus-value produced in his branch helps to regulate the average profit. But this is a process which occurs behind his back, one he does not see, or understand, and which indeed does not interest him. The actual difference of magnitude between profit and surplus-value - not merely between the rate of profit and the rate of surplus value - in the various spheres of production now completely conceals the true nature and origin of profit not only from the capitalist, who has a special interest in deceiving himself on this score, but also from the labourer. The transformation of values into prices of production serves to obscure the basis for determining value itself. III/9/165-166

BIBLIOGRAPHY

1. Arrow, K.J. and F.H. Hahn. General Competitive Analysis (London: Oliver & Boyd, 1972).

2. Baran, P.A. and P.M. Sweezy. Monopoly Capital (New York: Monthly Review Press, 1966).

3. Blackburn, R. (ed.). Ideology in Social Science: Readings in Critical Social Theory (London: Fontana-Collins, 1972).

4. Blaug, M. Ricardian Economics (New Haven, Conn.: Yale University Press, 1958).

5. Blaug, M. Economic Theory in Retrospect (2nd ed.) (London: Heinemann, 1968).

6. Bohm Bawerk. Karl Marx and the Close of his System. P. Sweezy (ed.). (London: Augustus Kelley, 1948).

7. Bortkiewicz, L. 'Value and Price in the Marxian System". J. Kahane (trans.) in A. Peacock (ed.) *International Economic Papers No. 2.*

8. Brown, Murray,O. A Measure of the Change in Relative Exploitation of Capital and Labour: *Review of Economics and Statistics,* May, 1966.

9. Carr, E.H. Socialism in One Country, 1924-26, Vol.I (London: Penguin, 1970).

10. Chambers, J.D. Enclosure and Labour Supply in the Industrial Revolution in *Economic History Review, Vol.V (1953).*

11. Coletti, L. 'Marxism: Science or Revolution?', in Rousseau to Lenin (London: New Left Books, 1973).

12. Deutscher, I. The Prophet Unarmed (London: Oxford University Press, 1970).

13. Dobb, M.H. Theories of Value and Distribution (London: Cambridge University Press, 1973).

14. Gillman, J. The Falling Rate of Profit: Marx's Law and its Significance to Twentieth Century Capitalism (London: Dobson, 1957).

15. Glyn, A. and R. Sutcliffe. British Capitalism, Workers and the Profit Squeeze (London: Penguin, 1972).

16. Godelier, M. "Structure and Contradiction in Capital", R.Miliband and J. Savile (eds.) The Socialist Register (London: Merlin Press, 1967).

17. Hobsbawm, E. Labouring Men (London: Weidenfeld and Nicholson, 1957)

18. Hyndman, H.M. "The Final Futility of Final Utility" in The Economics of Socialism (London, 1896).

19. Jones, A. The New Inflation (London: Penguin, 1973).

20. Kautsky, K. Die Agrarfrage.

21. Keynes, J.M. The General Theory of Employment, Interest and Money (London: Macmillan, 1961).

22. Klein, L.R. The Keynesian Revolution (2nd ed.) (London: Macmillan, 1966).

23. Lakatos, I. and A. Musgrave (ed.). *Criticism and the Growth of Knowledge* (Cambridge University Press, 1970).

24. Lenin, V.I. The Development of Capitalism in Russia (Moscow: Foreign Language Publishing House, 1956).

25. Leontief, W.W. Input-Output Economics (London: Oxford University Press, 1966).

26. Leijonhufvud, A. On Keynesian Economics and the Economics of Keynes (London: Oxford University Press, 1968).

27. Lipsey, R.G. An Introduction to Positive Economics (3rd ed.) (London: Weidenfeld and Nicholson, 1971).

28. Luxemburg, R. The Accumulation of Capital. A. Schwarzschild (trans. (London: Routledge and Kegan Paul, 1951).

29. Marx, K. Class Struggle in France (London: 1934).

30. Marx, K. Civil War in France (2nd ed.) (London)   1871).

31. Marx, K. Eighteenth Brumaire of Louis Bonaparte (New York   1898).

32. Marx, K. Wage-Labour and Capital (new ed.) (London: 1885).

33. Marx, K. Wages, Price and Profit (Peking: Foreign Language Press, (1965).

34. Mattick, P. Marx and Keynes (London: Merlin Press, 1971).

35. Meek, R. Studies in the Labour Theory of Value (2nd ed.) (London: Lawrence and Wishart, 1973).

36. Moore, B. The Social Origins of Dictatorship and Democracy (London: Penguin, 1971).

37. Morishima, M. Marx's Economics (Cambridge University Press, 1973).

38. Nicolaus, M. "The Unknown Marx", *New Left Review*, Vol. 48. (March-April, 1968).

39. Robinson, J. An Essay on Marxian Economics (London: Macmillan,1942).

40. Robinson, J. Economics of Imperfect Competition (London: Macmillan, 1933).

41. Samuelson, P. (1957). 'Wages and Interest: A Modern Dissection of Marxian Economic Models", *American Economic Review*, Vol. 47 (December 1957). pp. 884-912.

42. Samuelson, P. (1971). 'Understanding the Marxian Notion of Exploitation: A Summary of the so-called Transformation Problem between Marxian Values and Competitive Prices", *Journal of Economic Literature*, Vol.IX, ⧸ 2, (June 1971), pp. 399-431.

43. Shackle, G.C.S. "Keynes and Today's Establishment in Economic Theory: A View", *Journal of Economic Literature*, Vol.XI, ⧸ 2, (June 1973), pp. 516-519.

44. Sraffa, P. The Production of Commodities by Means of Commodities (London: Cambridge University Press, 1960).

45. Sweezy, P.M. The Theory of Capitalist Development (New York: Monthly Review Press, 1968).

46. Sweezy, P.M. (ed.) Karl Marx and the Close of his System (London: Augustus Kelley, 1948).

47. Sweezy, P.M. Some Problems in the Theory of Capital Accumulation. *Bulletin of the Conference of Socialist Economists*, (Autumn 1973), pp. 25-36.

48. Walker, A. "Karl Marx, the Declining Rate of Profit and British Political Economy", *Economica*, Vol.38, ⧸152, (November 1971), pp. 362-377.

49. Weiszacker, C. 'Morishima on Marx", *Economic Journal*, (forthcoming).

50. Wicksteed, P.H. The Commonsense of Political Economy (London: Routledge and Kegan Paul, 1944).